THE *bigbook* OF
environmental design

The twentieth century has experienced great changes and political, historical and social upheavals that have transformed humankind's everyday life. Technological advances have reshaped the tastes and habits of western society, and this has been reflected in art.

Architecture has not remained outside this process. It has evolved in such a way as to make the space more livable. In the nineties three factors stood out above the others: rapid and uncontrolled city growth, the awareness of the need to respect the environment, and the increased value of leisure time. The 'BigBook Of Environmental Design' shows how some of the best architects have found the way of meeting all these requirements while keeping the home functional.

In today's cities, green spaces have gradually been opened up so that humankind can stroll around on the grass and breathe in fresh air. Squares and parks have become the center of attention for the great designers of public spaces who have managed to merge asphalt with natural scenery. Urban parks have diversified the facilities they offer as people now seek to get more out of their leisure time.

More people out and about looking for ways of enjoying themselves has been a challenge for the architects. Two golf courses, a zoo and a mountain area are some of the examples of leisure architecture and landscape architecture selected in this book to show how intelligent and inspired design can satisfy the people as they play.

The 'BigBook of Environmental Design' shows all the fields in which architecture has been able to demonstrate the beauty it can create. Over the last years even civil engineering has evolved in its design, becoming more environment-friendly, and more eye pleasing. Any project - expressways, bridges, walls- is ideal to demonstrate the creativeness of what has been called 'landscape architecture'. This landscape is less rural and less natural than before the asphalt sprawl arrived, but it does not turn its back on the environment. Over the years designers of great projects are finding more sophisticated ways of reducing the inevitable impact a structure has on its setting. Many of these projects are due to a necessity. A building was needed for a specific role, however, the creators saw this as an opportunity to create a work of art.

Finally, the 'BigBook Of Environmental Design' deals with 'Land Art', architecture which vindicates the cause of enhancing the landscape. 'Land Art' appeared in the sixties and the seventies, gradually catching on over the years. Today its influence is felt on nearly all the projects at the turn of the century. This style of architecture perceives a commission as a means of transforming the panorama: when you gaze at it, you do not want to turn away. It bestows tranquility.

The plans and photographs with each project enable the reader to grasp the complexity of designing a construction in which beauty triumphs but functionality is not pushed aside. The 'BigBook of Environmental Design' offers you a general oversight of the projects in which the foremost architects have overcome landscape constraints to create beauty. The photographs take you through the latest trends in architectural art which have been attracting praise over the last decade, and will continue to do so.

URBAN SPACES

PARKS

BUILDINGS AND LANDSCAPE

LANDSCAPES OF RECREATION

CIVIL ENGINEERING AND RECLAIMING LAND

LAND ART

THE *bigbook* OF

environmental design

AUTHOR

Francisco Asensio Cerver

PUBLISHING DIRECTOR

Nacho Asensio

PROJECT COORDINATOR

Anna Puyuelo (Architect)

TRANSLATION & PROOFREADING

David Buss
Elaine Fradley

GRAPHIC DESIGN

Mireia Casanovas Soley
Noemí Blanco

LAYOUT

Jaume Martínez Coscojuela

TEXTS

Eduard Bru: Zoological Park.
Lorenzo Fernández-Ordóñez:
Intervention in the Caminito del Rey.
Maurici Pla: Introduction to Land Art. Le
Domaine du Rayol. Three Gardens in the Patios
of Telecenter Fyn Building. Kaze-no-Oka
Crematorium. Fuji Chuo Golf Club. Landscaping
of the A85 Freeway. The Concrete Garden.
Rubia Peregrina L. - Panel 0 m - Parc de
Gourjade. A Volume of Ligh- Jimmys.
Gisant/Transi.
Moisés Puente: Introduction to Landscapes
of Recreation. Schouwburgplein. Federal Court
Building Square, Minneapolis. Santo Domingo
de Bonaval Park. Plan for the Guadalupe River
Park. South Chula Vista Library Gardens.
Courtyards of the Ministry of Economy. Wakagi
Golf Club. Manliu Mountain Area. Uribitarte
Footbridge. Duisburg-Nord Park. Iceland Project
- Atlantik Wall - Dislocation. Storm King Wall -
Fieldgate - Road Stone - Herring Island.
Anna Puyuelo: Introduction to Urban
Spaces; Building & Landscape. Civil Engineering
and Reclaiming Land. HUD Plaza.
Borneo/Sporenburg. Ronda del Mig. Princesa
Sofía Park. River Congost Park. Acoustic Wall.
Parque do Tejo e Trançao.

Copyright © 2000 Francisco Asensio Cerver

Published by: Atrium International
Ganduxer 115, 4º
Barcelona 08022 Spain.
Phone +34-93-418 49 10 Fax +34-93-211 81 39
E-mail: arcoedit@idgrup.ibernet.com
Dep. Leg.: B-45462/99
ISBN: 84-8185-234-1
Printed in Spain

No part of this publication may be reproduced,
stored in retrieval systems or transmitted in any
form or by any means,
electronic, mechanical,
photocopying, recording or otherwise, without the
prior written permission of the owner of the copyright.

URBAN SPACES

The use of the term "landscape" to describe interventions in our cities is a relatively recent one. The former natural, bucolic meaning of the term has given way to a new definition; one that is perhaps more in accord with the realities of people's lives today, which are increasingly dominated by urban imagery. The term "urban landscape" seems to be a tacit acceptance of the loss of direct contact with the natural world, and suggests at the same time a new way of understanding cities and their public spaces.

Today, the objective is not to try and incorporate some caricaturized version of nature in civic spaces or to act radically in the opposite direction by completely eradicating any natural presence and presenting public spaces as something completely artificial in which even a tree seems out of place. It is now accepted that the artificiality of the urban landscape is something obvious which should not serve as a *leitmotif*, and as a result, the design of squares and urban spaces today incorporates a desire to improve people's quality of life in the broadest sense by trying to limit the traffic flow, provide space for play and other activities and above all, by ensuring that areas are connected internally.

The designs in this book, the majority of which have to deal with problematic pre-existing conditions, redefine, or as in the case of the design for Borneo-Sporenburg, define, the urban condition, so that it is not a mere residue, the inevitable result of other operations, but has a character of its own and is capable of generating life-enhancing environments in the middle of the city.

Martha Schwartz

Federal Court Building Square, Minneapolis

Federal Court Building Square lies in the center of Minneapolis, facing the old City Hall and lying at the foot of the new Federal Court Building itself, recently completed by the prestigious New York firm of Kohn, Pederson, Fox. The objectives of the commission were, firstly, to create a great civic space that reflected the overall nature of the city, and then if to provide a platform for the development of daily individual activities in a place capable of sustaining its own image and projecting its own sense of identity.

Few resources were used in the work, but their effectiveness is evident. Elements from the Minnesota landscape are placed in the Square in such a way that they acquire new values. These decontextualized elements become sculptures which evoke the familiar landscapes that form the shared experiences of the Minnesotans and symbolize both the natural landscape of the state and the changes it has undergone at the hands of mankind.

The most striking part of the design is a group of grass-covered tumuli, running from east to west, which have been planted with small indigenous pine trees of the type commonly found in the Minnesotan forests. These earth mounds are an echo of the undulating landscapes left behind in the area by glacial action and, like Japanese gardens, play with different scales, evoking both a mountainous landscape and, at the same time, a smaller-scale area covered in molehills.

The same intentions are obvious in the use of long tree trunks arranged as benches, which echo the traditional lumbering industry of Minnesota, one of the state's economic mainstays since its foundation. The aim is to remind people of familiar things and, by underlining the link between Minnesota and wood, to make this city-center square a gentler, more recognizable space in which familiarity breeds comfort.

These two main elements are supported by a neutral plane that resolves most of the Square. Banded paving, oriented towards the Federal Court Building, facilitates pedestrian movement and emphasizes the main entrance of the building. Where the tumuli themselves do not bar vehicular access, cubic stone pillars have been arranged to keep the Square traffic-free.

In the corners of the Square, the paving is interrupted by great circular metal grids which serve as air-conditioning outlets. Perimeter lighting illuminates the limits of the space, while embedded lights in the paving, aligned with the tumuli, light up the parallel faces of the mounds.

The new Square is sensitive to the harsh seasonal changes of Minnesota's weather. In winter, only the edges and central walkway of the space are visible through the snow, the rest of the Square being covered by footprints which zigzag between the tumuli, forming small paths similar to the tongues of a glacier. In spring and summer, the tumuli are a riot of color. Some are permanently covered by the green grass, while others are blanketed with white narcissi or blue lilies which mimic the blue bands of the paving.

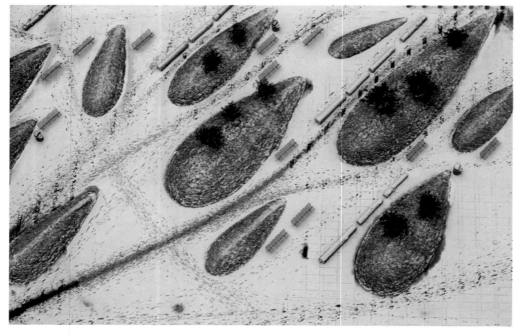

Aerial views of the plaza. In winter the pavement disappears and it is the footprints of the pedestrians which mark out the paths in the snow. The arrangement of the tumuli over the neutral plane of the ground makes for a zigzagging pattern between the mounds of earth and the wooden benches.

Location: Minneapolis, Minnesota, U.S.A.
Client: General Services Administration.
Surface area: 50,000 sq.ft.
Date: 1996.
Photographs: George Heinrich.

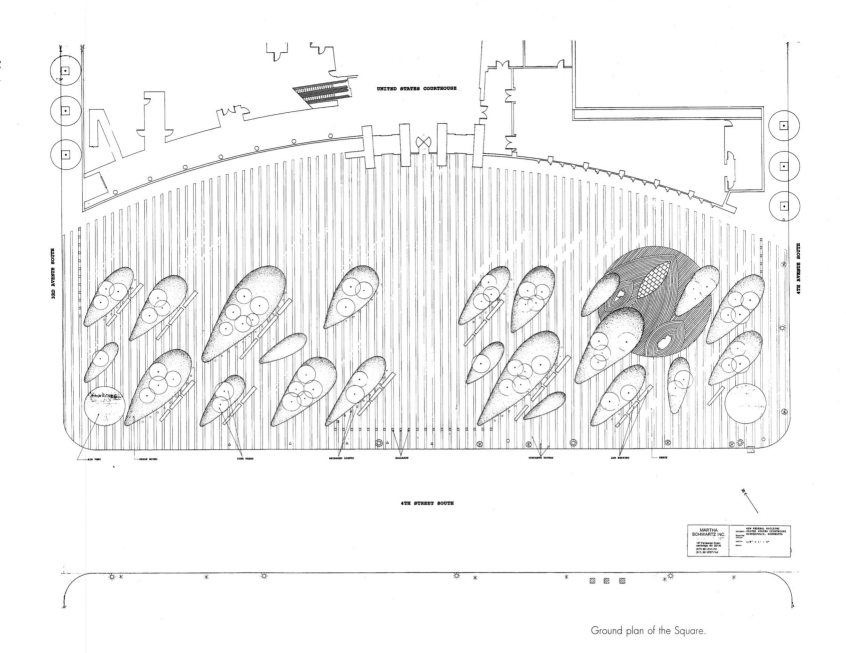

UNITED STATES COURTHOUSE

3RD AVENUE SOUTH

4TH AVENUE SOUTH

4TH STREET SOUTH

MARTHA SCHWARTZ INC.	NEW FEDERAL BUILDING UNITED STATES COURTHOUSE MINNEAPOLIS, MINNESOTA

Ground plan of the Square.

The small range of elements used to resolve the Square gives a very clear idea of what the design hopes to achieve, reinforcing the evocative effect. Both the tree trunks on the ground and the mounds of earth are visually powerful images capable of invoking familiar memories in the spectator, right in the heart of a big city.

14

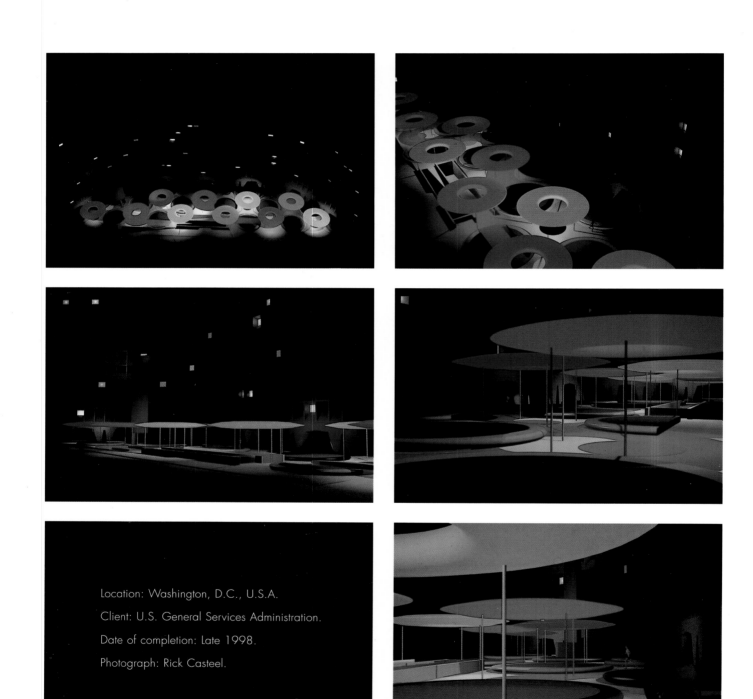

Location: Washington, D.C., U.S.A.
Client: U.S. General Services Administration.
Date of completion: Late 1998.
Photograph: Rick Casteel.

Martha Schwartz, Inc.

HUD Plaza

The space opposite the Department of Housing and Urban Development (HUD) in Washington D.C., designed by Marcel Breuer in 1968, was intended solely as a showcase for the building, and not to be used intensively by the building's 4,800 employees; at present, this urban desert is virtually unused. Adding to the desolation of the landscape is the base of the building, a dark stone wall which stands in the way of any visual connection between the space inside the building and the plaza.

This was the context of the commission that Martha Schwartz, Inc. received: to reactivate and make habitable the public space in front of a building which paradoxically houses the agency responsible for creating habitable spaces for people.

Schwartz's response is unconstrained by its urban context; it relies on its own arguments in an endeavor to give the place character and even get round the imposing presence of the building by constructing a plane which is suspended overhead: the boldly colored, lifesaver-shaped canopies.

The scheme repeats a circular motif measuring 30 feet in diameter in both the lower plane of planters and seats and the higher plane of differently colored canopies: vermilion, yellow and cobalt blue, recalling Breuer's own color palette for screens, walls and ceilings. The planters strike the note of plant life in a square built over an underground garage and therefore not designed to support the soil required to plant trees. Another circle in the form of diameter doubles as seating. The canopies and planters seem to float over the ground plane, an impression which is reinforced by the colored light arranged within. The canopies introduce a lightness of tone in contrast to the physical heaviness of the architecture beside them. The vinyl-coated plastic fabric canopies with their perforated circular shape are raised 14 feet above the ground, heightening the ethereal, floating impression they create, their other-worldliness which seems to be transposed to HUD Plaza for a few fleeting moments before returning to where they came from.

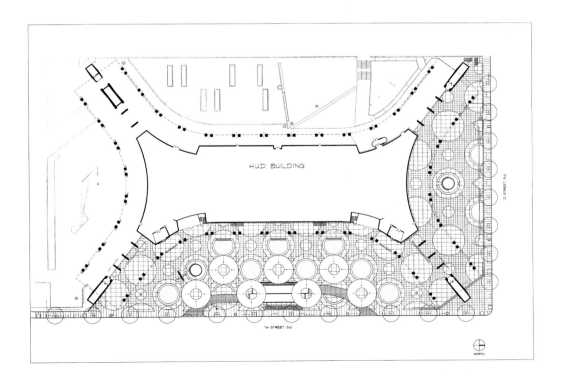

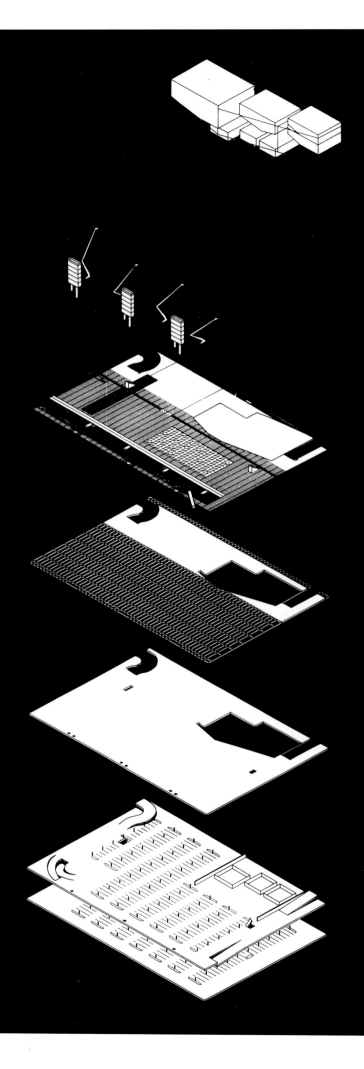

Schouwburgplein

Schouwburgplein occupies a prime site in the center of the Dutch city of Rotterdam. Surrounded by shops and offices and near to the central railway station, it constitutes one of the cultural centers of the city. As well as housing the municipal theater and a complex of concert halls, a new building holding a Pathé multi-screen cinema complex, designed by the architect Koen van Velsen, has recently been built.

However, what the architectural team of West 8 found when they began their project was a site without any defined character, excessively conditioned by the existence of an underground parking lot, which was in a very poor state, with some of the concrete on the point of collapse. A preliminary design by West 8, carried out in 1990, potentiated the qualities of the square as an agglutinating space for the city, laying down a new floor and completely renovating the parking lot. The final development of the square was radically changed in 1992 by the decision to build a new multi-screen cinema complex
in one corner, and the architects were asked to modify their design and adapt it to these new conditions. In fact, this change offered new possibilities of development, in particular the chance to dynamize the life of the square and the citizens occupying it.

With the city and its silhouette serving as both a backdrop and a physical limit, the basic objective of the design was to intensify the way the square was used. The design conserves the quality of an empty space that was central to the first design, and activates the horizontal plane by raising the floor of the square a foot above the level of the street. The square has been divided into different parts according to the changes in sunlight during the day, and different materials are used for the paving in each of them.

In the area that runs along the whole of the east side of the square, silver tree leaves have been embedded in a pavement of epoxy resin, while the east zone, which receives more sun throughout the day, has been given warmer materials such as wood and rubber, and was the logical site for a long bench. The obligatory ventilation shafts are supported by a 45 ft. high structure, and each shaft bears one of the hands —second, minute and hour— which go to make up a unique clock. Lastly, the central area, where there is the most activity, is paved with metal panels and contains an area of wooden toys which is a little more rugged.

The water and electric installations, a band of lights embedded in the ground and connections for stands for special events are all contained within the structure used to elevate the floor of the square. The peripheral ground lighting gives the sensation that the pavement is floating by blurring its limits. An additional attraction are four enormous hydraulic posts, more than 100 feet high, which assume different positions throughout the day, constantly changing the look of the square, and which can be maneuvred by onlookers by the simple expedient of placing a coin in a slot. In summer, there are water games for children which refresh the atmosphere. Pulverized jets of water spurt from below metal grills to fall on a granite pavement.

In Schouwburgplein, West 8 have succeeded in articulating a design by means of the changes that happen in the square itself: not only changes in the light, the weather or the seasons, but changes brought about by the direct action of the user. With the city as a backdrop, any action by its citizens in their new square becomes an event.

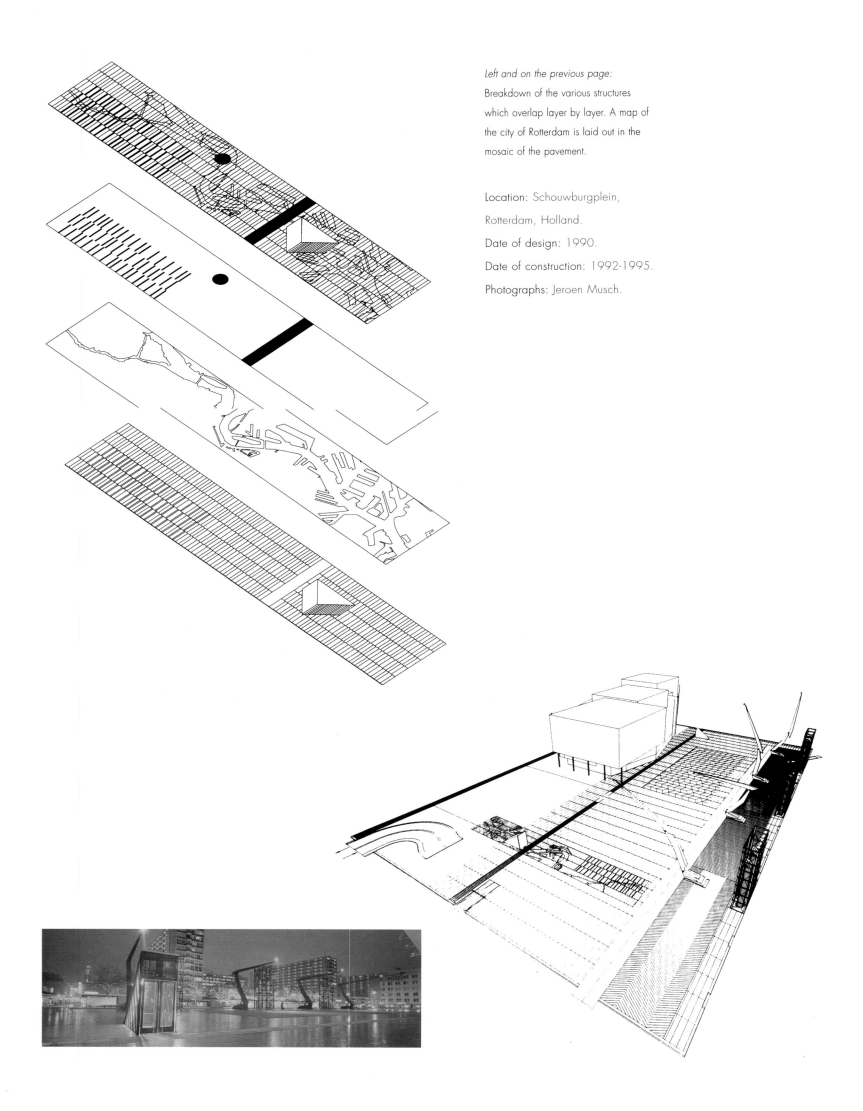

Left and on the previous page:
Breakdown of the various structures
which overlap layer by layer. A map of
the city of Rotterdam is laid out in the
mosaic of the pavement.

Location: Schouwburgplein,
Rotterdam, Holland.
Date of design: 1990.
Date of construction: 1992-1995.
Photographs: Jeroen Musch.

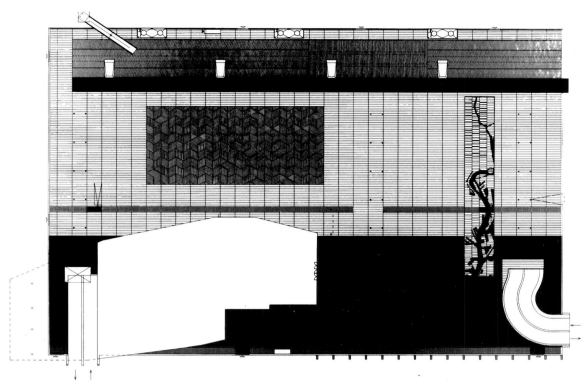

Ground level plan.

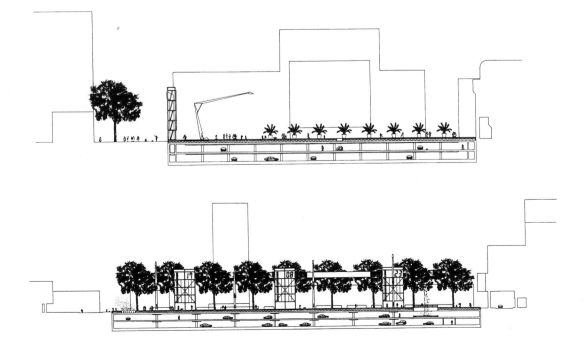

Longitudinal and cross sections. The pavement has been elevated a foot above street level.

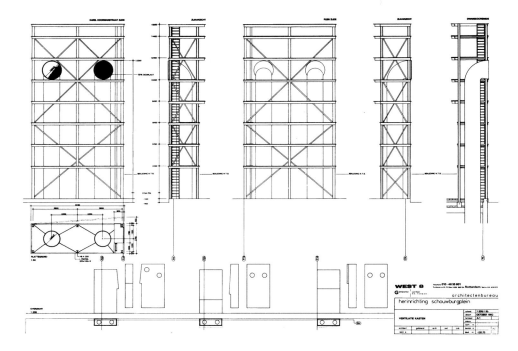

Detail of the ventilation shafts of the underground parking lot.

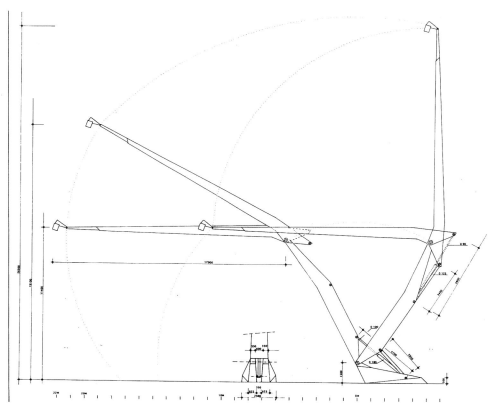

Articulated lamppost indicating the possible movements which can be controlled by the public.

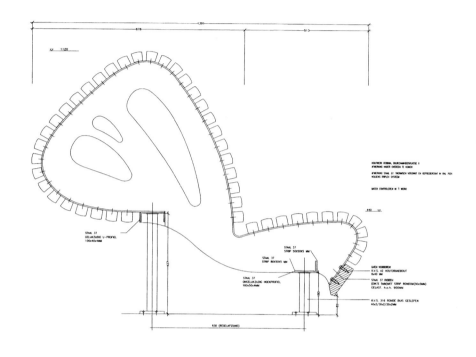

Long bench sited on the east side of the square
to make the most of the hours of sunlight.

The square acts as a stage
for the public.

Details of the points where
the different pavings meet.

Borneo/Sporenburg

The brief outlined for Borneo and Sporenburg (adjacent peninsulas in the eastern sector of Amsterdam's docks) had two requirements which were, in theory, diametrically opposed. On the one hand, these large docklands had to be exploited to the full for water-related activities. At the same time, paradoxically, these two docks were chosen for the construction of 2,500 homes in a low-level complex, equivalent to 100 homes per two and a half acres.

The challenge of uniting two such disparate aims presented a unique opportunity for urban experimentation. West 8, a Dutch team of landscape architects, came up with a solution by developing new types of three-story housing with direct access from the street, which would differ from normal houses in their relation to public and private space. The planned urban model is based on a strong relationship with private space in the form of patio and terraces. This is actually a variant on the typical Dutch house beside the canals, but with greater attention to privacy, reception of sunlight and shadow projection. The team created private areas in a great deal of what would usually be designed as public space, even within the site limits.

This basic model is manipulated and adapted to various types of home, including the two extremes of social housing and luxury homes. The team also wanted to create the utmost diversity of architecture as a change from the monotonous stretches of Borneo and Sporenburg with their anodyne single-family houses, all the same. The specific project for each housing group was commissioned to various architects who, as a starting point, were presented with larger building depths than usual: 16, 24, 26, 29 and 34 meters (defined by West 8 as the articulating mechanism of their idea). These depths allow the definition of new types of housing, with inner courtyards and/or ends which add to the spatial perception of the house, no matter how small. The inside-inside and outside-inside relationships multiply to accommodate the number of housing units stipulated in the brief, all with a real link to their surroundings, be it direct or merely visual.

The public space comprises 12-yard-wide streets marked out by user-friendly facades and house entrances; those on the perimeter are directly connected to the sea water. In addition to this low-density urban fabric, three large buildings with commanding profiles were designed, three landmarks in the area which can be seen from afar for easy orientation.

Although this is certainly not the first urban landscape operation of these proportions in the history of urban planning, it is encouraging, in a time of intensive property speculation, to find that there is still space for reflection and even investigation into new ways of living which are more in keeping with current lifestyles; Borneo and Sporenburg are the latest exponents of this current.

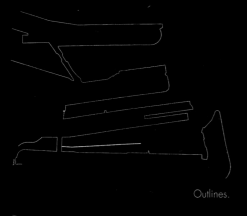

Outlines.

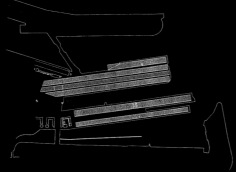

Urban fabric of low-density housing.

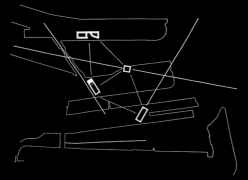

Sculptural blocks related to the landscape.

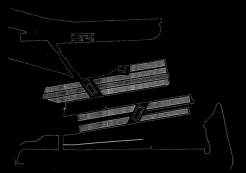

Superposition of all the elements.

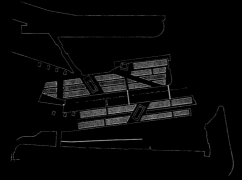

Definition of public space.

Location of the Borneo and Sporenburg
docks in the city of Amsterdam.

Location: Amsterdam, Holland.
Project date: 1993.
Construction: 1995-1998.
Photographs: Jeroen Musch.

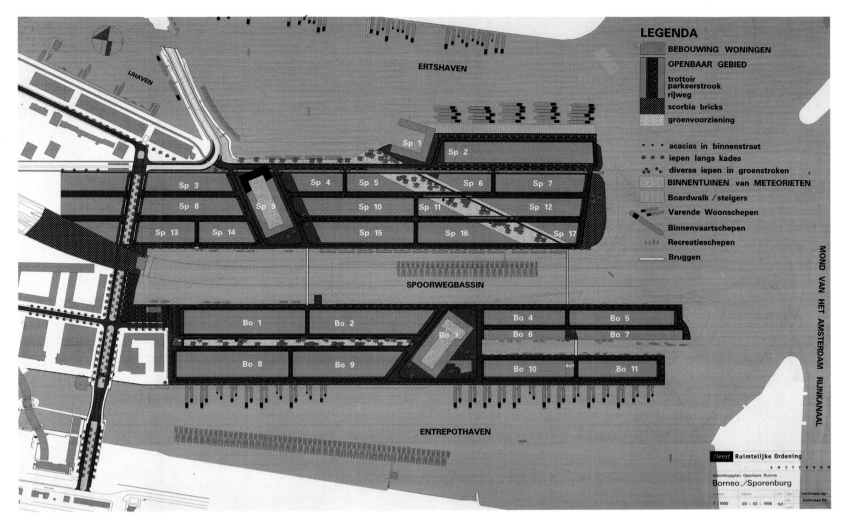

LEGENDA

▮	BEBOUWING WONINGEN
▮	OPENBAAR GEBIED
	trottoir
	parkeerstrook
	rijweg
▦	scorbia bricks
░	groenvoorziening

- · · · · acacias in binnenstraat
- ▪ ▪ iepen langs kades
- ♣ ♣ diverse iepen in groenstroken
- **BINNENTUINEN van METEORIETEN**
- ▬ Boardwalk / steigers
- ◣ Varende Woonschepen
- ▬ Binnenvaartschepen
- ◠◠◠ Recreatieschepen
- ── Bruggen

Typological points of departure:

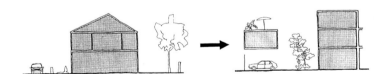

House with front and back
gardens: patio house.

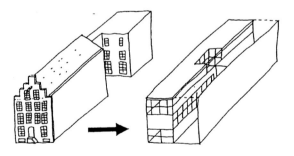

House beside the canal: patio house.

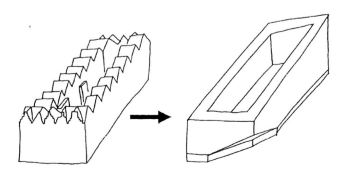

Urban block: sculptural block.

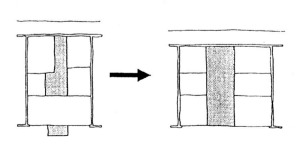

Common house: a loggia
completely open to light.

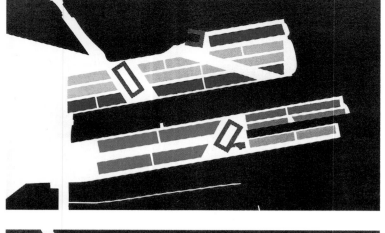

Depth of sites:
16, 24, 26, 29, 34 meters.

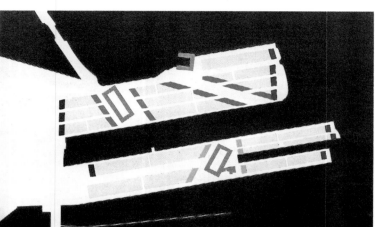

Differences in lifestyle: houses with
office, houses in plazas, introverted
houses and extrovert houses.

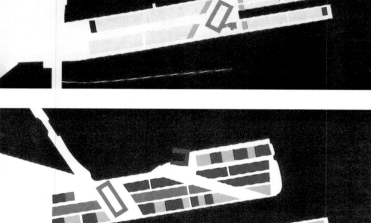

Brief: social housing, subsidized
housing, luxury housing.

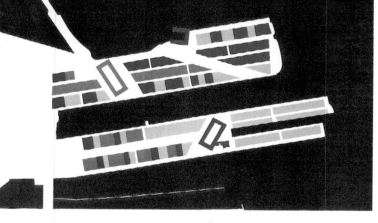

Developers: New Deal, Stichting
BO1, SFB, Smits Bouwbedrijf,
Bouwbedrijf M.J. de Nijs en zonen,
individuals.

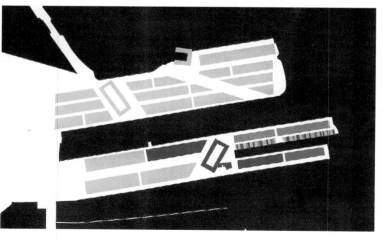

Architects taking part in the operation: Stephane Beel, Van Berkel & Bos, DKV, FARO,
Xaveer de Geyter, Heren 5, Steven Holl, Inbo, JA Atelier, Claus & Kaan, Marge,
W. J. Neutelings, OMA Rem Koolhaas, Rowin Petersma, Höhne & Rapp, Marlies Rohmer,
Köther & Salman, Tangram, Van Sambeek & Van Veen, Ruth Visser, H. Zeinstra,
Kees Christiaanse, Herzog & de Meuron, LRRH, Mastenbroek en Van Gameren,
Van Herk en De Kleyn, Mateo, EEA, Steven Sorgdrager, Koen van Velsen,
Liesbeth van der Pol, Tupker en Van de Neut, CASA, Van Goor, Stuurman & Partners.

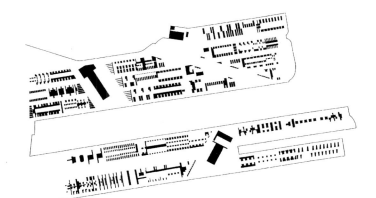

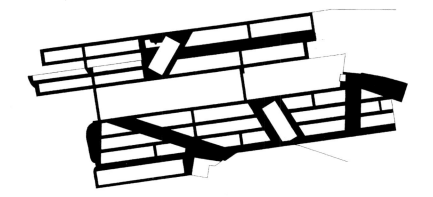

The brief upscales private life and
downscales public space.

Views of different blocks of housing in the Borneo-Sporenburg area, under construction. The variety and diversity of facades was one of the project's conditions, and was guaranteed by the long list of architects involved in designing these housing blocks.

Jordi Henrich & Olga Tarrasó

Ronda del Mig

Barcelona's Ronda del Mig is virtually an urban motorway, which, when constructed, was designed to act as a peripheral beltway to connect the northeast and southwest ends of the city. Over time, urban expansion has seen it become firmly embedded in the modern city, with housing blocks lining both its sides. For almost all its length, the Ronda del Mig slashes through the city, impeding communications between the two sides and polluting the lives of the adjoining neighbors with its noise. The situation was so bad that it gave rise to energetic protests and demands that the road should be covered, from the people living alongside the stretch of the road that was the object of this actuation.

The project consisted of covering the Ronda's traffic lanes with an underground parking lot, and then covering the whole work to form a central pedestrian precinct, thus creating a public space over what used to be an insuperable barrier. The lateral lanes were also redesigned, widening the pavements and reducing the traffic lanes to two each side, with no facilities for parking.

The area created above the parking lot has been designed as a pedestrian walkway some 90 feet wide, divided into a central lane of 22 feet and two lateral bands of 30 feet which contain trees and areas of lawn, and which rise and fall to allow access. These two lateral bands are raised above the adjoining traffic lanes in a clear attempt to separate the pedestrian area from the traffic. This height difference varies between 6.2 feet in the areas that are grassed over and 2.6 feet where there are access ramps. At both ends of the precinct, and where it crosses Carrer Miguel Àngel, smooth gradients bring it down to the level of the traffic. In contrast, the other lateral accesses are composed of ramps which are situated at the entrances to the parking lot and at pedestrian crossings.

The new design breaks the constant section that was configured by the buildings and the previous road layout, and at the same time resolves many urban and communication problems. The cross section changes, allowing the spectator to appreciate the variation and movement thus created. The changes in height may be smooth or abrupt, the street lighting moves from one side to the other and varies in its size and orientation, the areas of lawn are not continuous bands, but are interrupted to give access or for the groupings of trees in large planters.

As this is a concrete structure, care had to be taken to prevent too heavy a load in the form of vegetation. So the mimosa, tipuana and date palm trees which line the central walkway are either contained in the above-mentioned planters of sheet steel, or situated in the areas of lawn. The drainage systems are interconnected and are also linked to the main drains.

Sheet steel, a material relatively little used in public spaces, acts as the common denominator of the different elements of urban decoration; the lampposts specially designed for this project, the railings, the balustrade-type benches, the anti-parking bollards, the borders of the lawns and of course the great planters for the trees.

Location: Ronda del Mig
(between the Carretera de Sants and
Avinguda Madrid), Barcelona.
Surface area: 27,140 sq.yds.
Client: Barcelona City Council.
Associates: Ramón Cardona,
Jordi Carulla and Juan Corominas
(technical architects).
Date of design: 1995-1996.
Date of completion: 1997.
Photographs: Josep Maria Molinos +
David Cardelús/Wenzel.

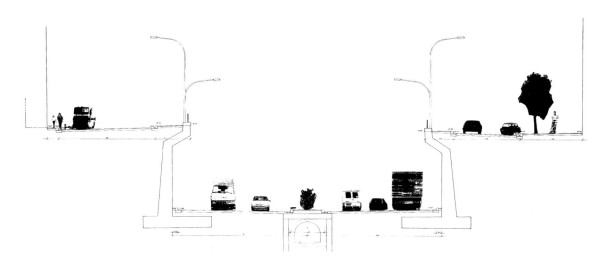

Cross section before the project.

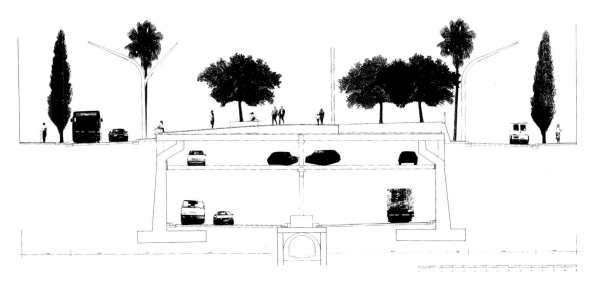

Cross section of the design.

The promenade is paved with black and deep red slabs which form patterns that combine with the areas of lawn. The slabs in the central promenade are placed longitudinally and measure 12 x 20 x 2.5 inches, while those in the lateral bands measure 20 x 20 x 2.5 inches. Steel is used for other elements of urban decoration, except for the granite used for the pedestrian crossings and the borders which are slabs of artificial stone measuring 20 x 20 x 2 inches.

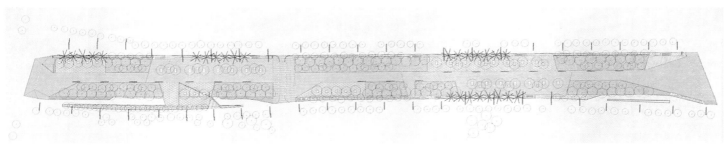

General plan.

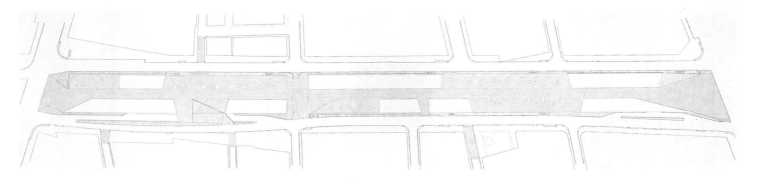

Paving.

Lighting.

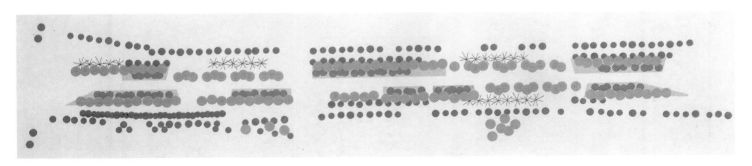

Trees. Position and species.

Communication between the two sides is at ground level at the two ends of the promenade and where it is crossed by Carrer Miguel Àngel. Vehicle access is limited by steel bollards. The other means of access to the central promenade are the ramps which coincide with the pedestrian crossings.

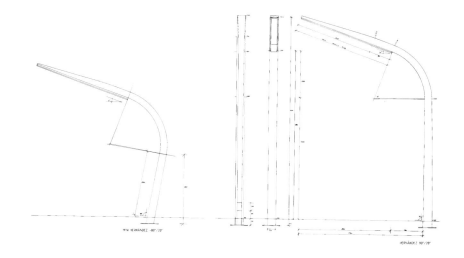

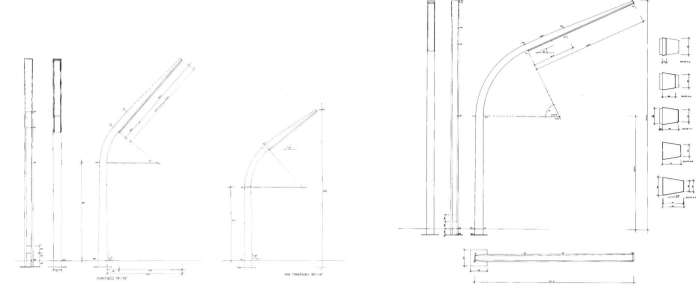

Support for the lighting.

Bruno Fortier & Italo Rota

Public Spaces in the Center of Nantes

The work of Bruno Fortier and Italo Rota was a response to a competition organized by Nantes City Council in 1991 to come up with a project for the rehabilitation of a large area of public space in the city center. At the time it was occupied by a large area of car parking and the remains of commercial and, in places, military uses related to the two rivers which form these large urban spaces: the Loire and the Erdre. The area covered by the project occupies two major axes joined in a T-shape: the broad section including the Île Feydeau in a tributary of the Loire, running from east to west, and a perpendicular axis which is the old river bed of the Erdre, and is now occupied by the Cours des Cinquante Otages.

While the object of the competition was to come up with an overall plan to organize all of these areas, to date only the Cours des Cinquante Otages has been built, leaving the remaining area, known as the Île Verte, still at the planning stage.

Fortier and Rota took the history of these places and their relation to city history as the basis for their work, contrasting them with the present-day and future needs of the city of Nantes. They picked up on the fact that these large spaces were open and extensive, "a great empty space", to create a design which would respect their lightness and spaciousness. They were therefore dealing with a far more extensive area of land than is normally understand by the term urban space, but one which was subject to ordinances which discriminated against their uses and controlled the course of the various objects which were to circulate around them. The urban furniture and all the related accessories had to create quite a different atmosphere to the desolation of disorder and adapt to the functional needs of the present-day city-machine with its circulation, its flows, and all the demands of transport which have to be met.

In dealing with motor traffic, the project opted for a very strict, tightly controlled channeling with dimensions (widths, turning arcs, etc.) adapted to a measured idea of traffic on the scale of the overall life of the city. In the Cours des Cinquante Otages, the road forms a very strict channel which uses the characteristic procedures of traffic incorporation to pick up the adjacent routes, with a return to the time-honored roundabout to facilitate access and exit at junctions. Motor traffic is not segregated from other urban sectors because of speed or belonging to a larger-scale network; it is integrated harmoniously as one more cog in the workings of the overall urban space.

The tram lines are treated in the same way and combine their flow with pedestrian areas and roads without producing any interference. Fortier and Rota's project for the Cours des Cinquante Otages is based on a harmonious, compatible integration of the three flows: pedestrian, motor traffic and tram lines.

All the props used for these functions in the form of urban furniture (lighting, tram shelters and stops, etc.) is used to introduce elements of order into the vast extension of space, and this is achieved by recourse to series and alignments of elements. The same can be applied to the trees: the project returns to Nantes' old tradition of magnolia trees to recreate an urban atmosphere that takes its cue from the past, though updated; the series and alignments of trees (with their variations, changes of rhythm, etc.) combine with the ordering of other elements in an attempt to recreate an atmosphere which is both urban and well spaced out.

The proposal put forward by this project has the great merit of endeavoring to combine an idea of city which picks up the values of the nineteenth century city, further improved by techniques of organization in keeping with a traditional conception of architecture and urban planning. The city of Fortier and Rota will be a city of civitas, of urbane atmosphere and harmonious co-existence: quite the opposite of the values advocated by the new metropolitan scale which has so enamored recent generations of architects.

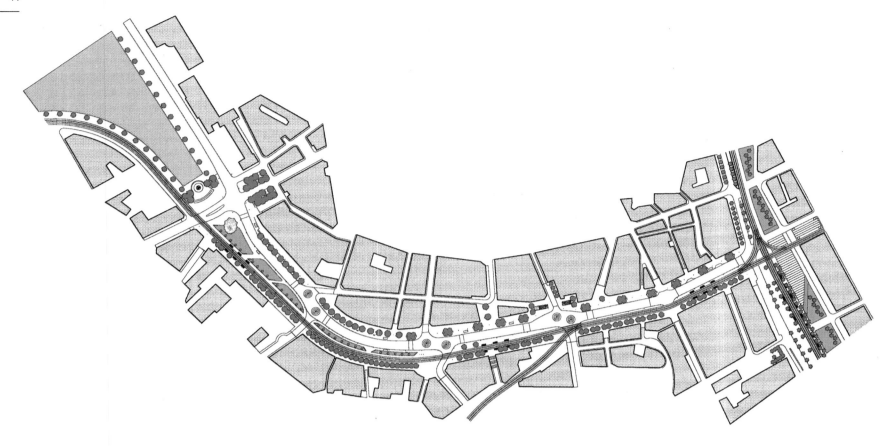

In 1994, of the whole project for public
spaces, only the part corresponding to
the Cours des Cinquante Otages had
been built on the old river bed of the Erdre,
which follows a north-south line to join
up with the "Île verte" at its southern extreme.

Location: Nantes, France.
Client: Nantes City Council.
Collaborators: Jean-Thierry Bloch
(engineer), Roger Narboni (lighting),
Jean-Claude Hardy (landscape architect).
Competition date: 1991.
Construction date (1st phase): 1992-1994.
Photographs: Phillippe Ruault.

The urban furniture (trees, lamp posts, paving, etc.) is laid out according to alignments and series which impose order on a space which at no moment renounces its extension or the generosity of its dimensions.

The organization of public space is based on a system which combines pedestrian, tram and motor traffic routes in a complex where they all function harmoniously with no need for segregation, in keeping with a conception of city rooted in the past.

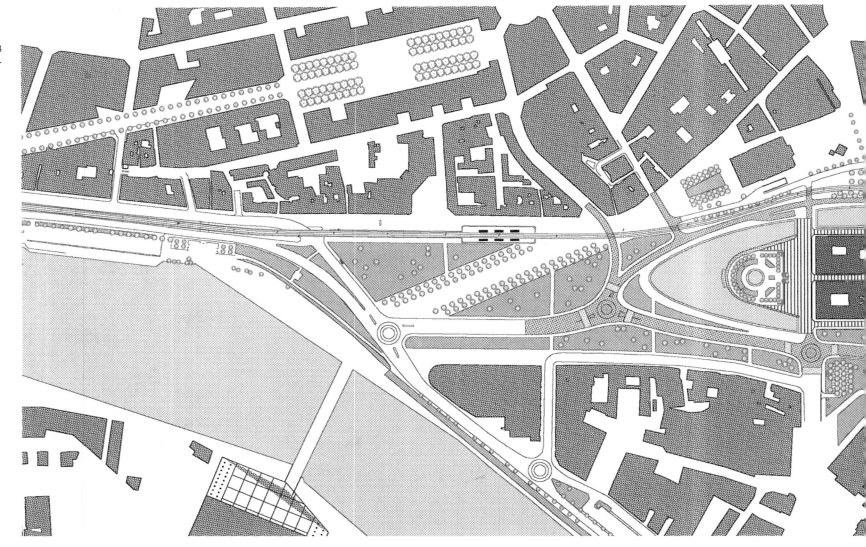

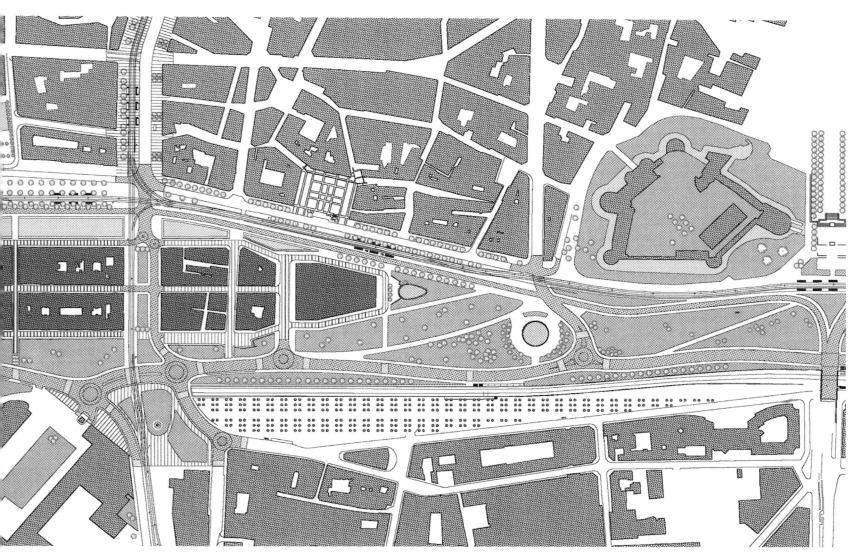

Layout of the design for
the L'Île Verte area.

Current state.

PARKS

Today's public parks –defined areas containing a determined form of more or less artificially manipulated nature– have their genesis in the picturesque parks and recreation areas which came into vogue during the closing stages of the eighteenth century. At that time, public spaces had a defined social function: they were merely the stages for politics, religion or the holding of markets. Never before had public areas been seen as vehicles for the promotion of leisure, health or contact with nature.

However, the industrial revolution, which brought about huge demographic changes and a rapid growth in the size of cities, also created the need to specifically create public spaces destined for leisure use and to provide some form of direct contact with nature.

In other words, public parks were a direct result of the rise of the new urban, democratic industrialized society, whose citizens for the first time in history did not have this direct and close contact with the natural world.

Today, the same situation pertains, although the circumstances have varied a little. If there are still a large number of people for whom parks are the only practical means of escaping in some degree from the city, the increasingly media-based nature of the leisure industry has influenced the use of these areas. In an age when people's free time is increasingly dominated by television and expensive theme parks, etc., the role of public parks is changing. Many of them now program cultural and sporting activities as a response to these changes, as our public spaces rethink their function, trying to adapt to the needs of the end of the century.

Atelier Acanthe & Gilles Clément

Le Domaine du Rayol

Le Domaine du Rayol occupies a particularly beautiful part of the Côte des Maures on the French Mediterranean coast between the villages of Canadel and Cavalaire, a few miles from St. Tropez. In 1989, the area of about 12.5 acres was bought by the Conservatoire du Littoral, who commissioned Clément with its landscaping. Previously, the terrain had been in the hands of various private owners who had left some signs of occupation and attempts at development. These included the Hôtel de la Mer, a farm and a villa, as well as a pergola and a series of paths which cover the whole area. Clément decided to conserve all these elements, with the exception of some hangers previously used for the construction of airforce weaponry during World War II, which were demolished.

Clément's proposal to the conservation body was the creation of a "Southern Garden", a concept which the designer himself defined as "a complex of the compatibility of life". This meant a space where the authentic inhabitants were the flora planted there and which could become a place for experimenting with the behavior of different species and their relation with one another and with the climate. Clément divided the terrain into different sectors, each corresponding to a different region or country: Australia, New Zealand, Tasmania, South Africa, Chile, Mexico, California and China.

Many of the species which were planted during the six years of work needed to set up the garden were in fact found in Europe, although some had to be brought from their countries of origin or grown from seed. All the work involved was carried out on site and included an experimental tracking of how each species behaved. The proposal was to create a garden that would promote an understanding of the plant world by a process of dislocation and relocation in Le Domaine, following the universal method of taking an organic element out of its original context and trying to maintain its vitality as one of the best ways of understanding its nature. Clément calls Le Domaine "a garden for understanding", a place where the vitality and growth of the vegetation are protagonists.

Clément and his associates carried out all the work on site, as the project was oriented by the strict logic of the cohabitation of the various species and their relation with the environment: the humidity, the sun, the composition of the soil, the rocks and the development of the roots. These variables guided the different decisions taken as to planting, with the species in the different sectors being put to the test when located in a context of cohabitation, namely the "complex of the compatibility of life" that the Southern Garden constitutes.

The result of Clément's intervention is far from the accepted notions of landscape architecture, but also from those of garden architecture. He does not seek to create landscapes in the sense of pictures or scenes prepared for human view, nor is his work governed by a criteria of order that makes the garden appear to be designed or conceived for human habitation. It can instead be seen as an operation of "planned and ordered reforestation" in the sense that the transplanted species are cleary independent of the colonizing experience of man, which is represented by the existing structures: the hotel, the pergola, the paths and the straight stairway. However, the garden is also differentiated from nature in the raw by the fact that it is the hand of man –the gardener– who is charged with caring for and understanding the life of these species. In this way, the nature of Le Domaine, halfway between the unfettered vitality of nature and the tenuous sense of harmony which can only result from human activity, results in a possible landscape which demonstrates the highest level of planning: minimal human interference which improves and channels the raw vitality characteristic of the plant world.

Various view of the original landscape.
Although there are plants from other
countries, they were already growing
here when work started on the project.

Location: Le Rayol Canade, France.

Client: Conservatoire du Littoral.

Surface area: 12.5 acres.

Landscape architect: Gilles Clément,
Philippe Deliau.

Conservation: François Macquart-Moulin.

Gardeners: Jean-Laurent Felizia,
Jean-Michel Battin.

Importations: Albert Tourrette.

Starting date: 1988.

Completion date: 1997.

Photographs: Alexandre Bailhache.

The stone and wood pergola and the long, straight-lined starway are two elements which existed on the site prior to 1989, when Le Domaine du Rayol was purchased by the Conservatoire du Littoral to be landscaped. These two elements are the basis of the composition.

Le Domaine du Rayol is divided into eight sectors which correspond to different areas of the planet: Australia, New Zealand, Tasmania, South Africa, Chile, Mexico, California and China. On this page, various views of the New Zealand sector: a meadow of yellow Carex and Leptospemos.

Le Rayol is conceived as a garden by the sea, but no one which is laid out according to criteria of architecture or even landscaping, with a view to preparing vistas for a potential human eye. Human intervention on the laws of natural plant growth is stricthy limited to the realm of gardening.

The nothern sector of the plot holds the Australian garden with its Black Boys, black-trunked trees which are fire-resistant when burnt on the surface.

Above:
South African flora in
front of the pergola.

These groves of fan palms, natives of
the American tropics, stand out from the
compact landscape of local species.
The stream was cleared and planted
with shade-loving species.

The higher Land is marked by a typical Mexican-style desert landscape. The largest trees in this garden are a variety of yuca.

Le Domaine du Rayol is conceived as a Southern Garden by the sea, where species from different parts of the planet cohabit in a "complex of compatibilities", marked by diversity and the protagonism of the plants themselves.

Above:
The sector devoted to China has preserved the existing bamboos, which are joined by sago palms from the same country.

The underwater landscape (sea garden) can be visited with a ghide who specializes in sea plants and animals.

Atelier Acanthe & Gilles Clément

Henri Matisse Park

The project for this urban park on the outskirts of Lille is marked by Clément's interest in the relationships established between different plant species and with the human habitat. It creates a series of areas each with its own concept expressed in its name, with each concept expressing a specific organizational order of flora and the link visitors to the park establish with it.

This subdivision of the vast area covered by the park produces three main sectors: the Place de l'Europe, a paved enclosure which joins up to the Viaduc Le Corbusier; Le Boulingrin with its great grassy square covered with flowers in the center; and the Bois des Transparences et des Clarières, a wood punctuated with clearings, each with its own thematic aspect. A final important element, bordering the grassy square and the wood, is the Ille Derborence. This area is raised some five meters above the surrounding ground and contains an abundant array of deciduous autumnal vegetation. This area is only open to scientists, as a laboratory in which to study species, set apart from human activity, where plant life can live and grow independently.

The idea behind Le Boulingrin is to represent the actual park, which is open on all sides, with its lush plant life. Access to the Bois des Transparences is also completely free; here there are four clearings (four open spaces, or absences of vegetation) expressed by four references to this absence: marshland, fire, the wind that bends trees, and moor. Clément has chosen a specific expression for each topic: fire is expressed by a fire-resistant species, and wind by the planting of wind-bowed trees.

On the borders of these two sectors is the Ille Derborence, a small-scale replica of an island that exists in the real world: the island of Antipode. Clément describes it thus: "This is a real inhabited sanctuary in nature. Only scientists visit there on short, sporadic forays. It is on a similar latitude to Lille and has a harsh, damp, cold climate under the direct influence of the Antarctic climate. There are no trees there: the wood is reduced to scrubby brushwood, bowed down by the winds off the sea. The opposition of the 'expressions of life' which correspond to a single binomial takes on its full force here."

Clément gives the Ille Derborence the same outline as Antipode —though inverting and downscaling it–, and raises it five meters higher than the grassy square, banking it with a great stone wall, like a fortress. He sees it as an untouched system that represents a world before man's appearance, which man should contemplate in its virgin state, as he, too, ultimately belongs to it. The species planted in Derborence are taken from very varied places on the planet in an attempt to follow a much-loved concept of Clément's: all the planet's species could be brought to co-exist in a single system. This is a concept that also found expression in his project for Le Domaine du Rayol.

Visitors to the park can enter Derborence by means of a small stairway that starts in Le Boulingrin and leads to the center of the island; here, through a glass cover, as outsiders, they can view many species which have already disappeared from their native habitats, and have been introduced and revitalized on the island by the expert hands of scientists.

Henri Matisse Park represents another step forward in Clément's interest in insisting on the binomial between man and the autonomous life of the plant kingdom, and seeing the life of each plant species as an integral part of a system which covers the entire planet. The Euralille complex is a real theme park where the planet's plant world is displayed and studied, representing aspects of information and research. It is a park of symbols and realities, where the experience of the traditional city park becomes compatible with immersion in a city made up of all the inhabitants of the plant kingdom. These inhabitants may be special species and samples, but Clément hopes that they can also live out their full lives in relation to the place, the climate and their fellow inhabitants.

Location: Lille, France.

Client: Lille City Council.

Surface area: 20 acres.

Associates: Empreinte (Eric Berlin, Sylvain Plipo,

Axelle Veynacques), Claude Courtecuisse.

Date of competition: 1992.

Photographs: Eric Berlin.

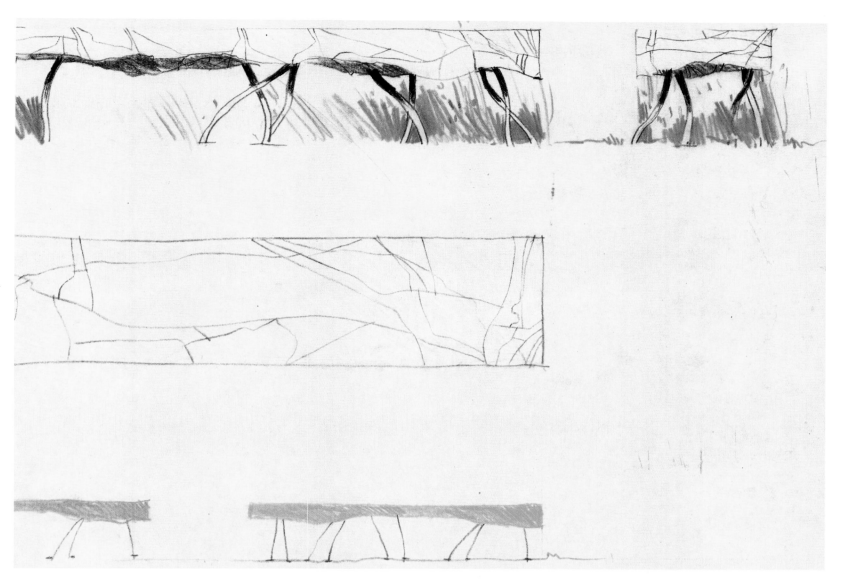

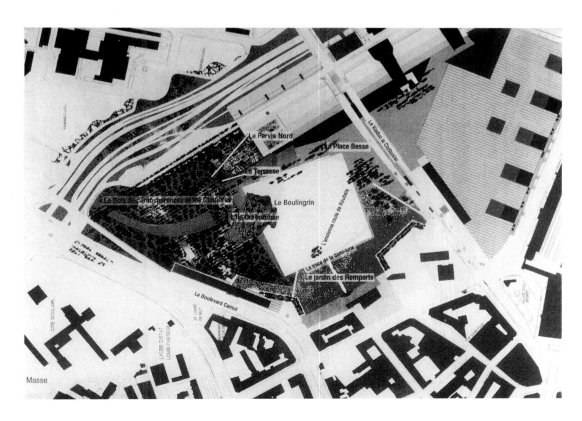

Clément gives the Ille Derborence the same outline as Antipode —though inverting and downscaling it—, and raises it five meters higher than the grassy square, banking it with a great stone wall, like a fortress. He sees it as an untouched system that represents a world before man's appearance, which man should contemplate in its virgin state, as he, too, ultimately belongs to it. The species planted in Derborence are taken from very varied places on the planet in an attempt to follow a much-loved concept of Clément's: all the planet's species could be brought to co-exist in a single system.

Alvaro Siza Vieira & Isabel Aguirre

Santo Domingo de Bonaval Park

The convent of Santo Domingo de Bonaval enjoys a splendid position on a hill to the north of the city of Santiago. Here, in the walled enclosure formerly belonging to the convent, Alvaro Siza has built the Galician Center of Contemporary Art and the park presented on these pages, and is designing a building to house the Eugenio Granell Foundation Museum on one edge of the park.

The Park de Bonaval, with a surface area of 378,000 sq. ft., occupies the grounds of the convent, founded in the thirteenth century, which is divided into three clearly differentiated areas: a terraced vegetable garden at the lowest part near the new museum, an old oak grove and a cemetery on the higher ground which has not been used since it was closed down in 1934. The abandoned, overgrown estate was gradually developed as clearing work advanced, varying the planned scheme according to the parts laid bare. The task of transforming such a unique setting into a public park called for a respectful treatment of the existing elements: tumble-down walls, ruins, paths, tombs and, above all, stone and water. Old convent documents revealed that this area was the source for old fountains and washing places in the north of the city. The streams and sources were cleared to allow the water to follow its old course, this time to bring life to the park itself. Fountains, small channels of water which rise and disappear, piles of stone and brooks running from the oak grove to the old vegetable garden, crossing paths and leaping walls, making the grass and the moss between the stones grow.

Recovery work in each area was carried out with the greatest attention to existing elements. A small geometric garden attached to the convent was known to exist in the low area of the vegetable garden, and was restored. The rest of the layout has been preserved, respecting the original intelligent distribution of platforms on different levels, all communicated by ramps. One of these platforms, in the middle of a green meadow, serves as a natural plinth for a sculpture by Eduardo Chillida, The Door of Music, which stands against the outer wall. Rundown outbuildings complete this strongly sloping terraced area. The oak grove has preserved every one of its trees. The emptier upper stretch will be the venue for the future head office of the Eugenio Granell Foundation Museum. Winding old paths that led up and down the terraces were recovered, and the transition ramps planted with bushes to emphasize their course. One of these paths passes under a lych gate carved with the letter omega leading into the cemetery. The higher land respects the original layout of lines of graves. A large meadow with paths and a few old trees presents splendid vistas over the convent of Santo Domingo de Bonaval to a skyline dominated by the cathedral spires, a view which was hitherto inaccessible to the citizens of Santiago. Where the higher ground of the cemetery borders on rather unattractive land beyond, trees were planted to provide greater seclusion without blocking views of the city. On the lower ground of the graveyard, beside the apses of the church, the stone niche structures are preserved as witnesses of the park's previous life.

The materials and methods used demonstrate the extreme care taken with the work. Rather than canceling out the old, the new materials endeavor to blend in. In fact the same materials are used —granite, grass, moss, water— to the extent that the combination of the two, with no attempt at falsification, continues practically the same as before. In such a rainy city as Santiago, it is the grass and moss that grow over everything and unite the three very different parts of the park. All the connections between them already existed; here they are merely uncovered and shown to us. The project for the park, which was actually designed after the museum, appears to respond perfectly not just to the extraordinary character of the place, but to the museum itself, which seems like a summerhouse in a perfect symbiosis of the two projects.

Location: Rúa da Caramoniña,

Santiago de Compostela, Spain.

Client: Santiago de Compostela City Consortium.

Surface area: 378,000 sq. ft.

Collaborators: Alessandro D'Amico, Xorxe Nuno

and Carlos Muro.

Project date: 1990-1994.

Completion date: 1994.

Photograph: Tino Martínez.

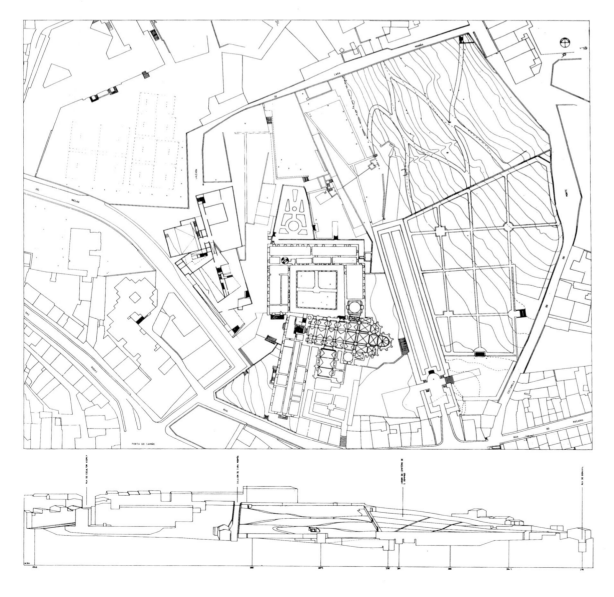

General plan of the Santo Domingo de Bonaval complex containing the Centre of Galician Contemporary Art, the old convent and the park, whose three zones are perfectly delimited. The cemetery and the oak wood are in the upper part and the old vegetable garden of the convent lies next to the new museum in the lower part.

The low ground of the park, occupied by the convent's old vegetable plots, preserves its terraced structure. A geometric garden which has been reconstructed on one of them used to lead directly to the cloister of the convent. A sculpture by E. Chillida, The Door of Music, is set in a meadow on one of the terraces.

A system of ramps connects the terraces of the vegetable garden and communicates with the higher land near the oak grove.

The high ground of the vegetable gardens preserves the remains of old outhouses and leads to the oak grove. As the path climbs, different views of the old city center are revealed.

The area of the cemetery conserves traces of the old paths between the graves. In the upper part, which is in contact with the exterior, new trees have been planted which do not obstruct the view of the silhouette of the city with the towers of the cathedral. The stone structures of the graves are conserved as a reminder of the former use of the park.

José Antonio Martínez Lapeña
Elías Torres Tur

Princesa Sofía Park

The main aim of this project to remodel the park is based on respect for and reassessment of its trees in the form of a new layout. The complex is organized around four strips of sinuous forms which follow the lines of the park's palm trees, planted between the grassy areas and surrounded by Corten iron plates. More palm trees were planted to fill in the empty spaces, thereby forming continuous rows. The strips run from north to south right across the park. The spaces between them take the form of more, similar strips, paved with fine white earth, containing a haphazard collection of other trees.

Two straight streets, also running north-south, are superposed on them; these avenues are asphalted to make the vast park more accessible for traffic. The street to the west borders a rectangular strip running parallel to Calle 20 de Abril, where the original Information and Tourism Office building is preserved and the existing service buildings are to be remodeled to create a new grouping, which is not included in this project.

Another winding street, also asphalt-surfaced and broader than the others, making it the main axis of activities inside the park, crosses it from east to west. It is lined by a eucalyptus grove to make the most of the closeness of the phreatic level, turning it into an avenue and a particularly suitable spot for the annual fair in La Línea. This avenue interrupts the strips of grass in its passage, but not the sinuous rows of palm trees.

With a view to providing a greater variety of itineraries around the park and making its many corners more accessible, a series of three-meter-wide paths have been drawn out, running parallel to the main street-promenade and crossing the strips of grass at regular intervals.

To the south of the eucalyptus grove stand two concrete buildings which provide venues for open-air shows: a stage with rows of tiered seating, set between changing rooms and one of the east-west paths, and a rectangular pavement with tiered seating along its longest side. Two great canopies, also made of concrete, extend lengthwise beside the two constructions and next to the central esplanade to provide shelter for the kiosks and bars which are set up here from time to time. The park's four fortifications have been respected and pointed up by their situation on the strips of grass.

The park is rounded by a path of large concrete slabs in which hollows are sunk for two rows of palm trees, except on the side which gives onto Calle 20 de Abril, which provides the visual limit and outer promenade with no further physical enclosures.

An area has been left free, with no interventions, on the eastern side; this is the site for the hotel planned to complete the ideas competition, and is therefore not included in this initial phase.

A combined system has been installed for the lighting and watering of the park. A series of giant sprinklers are hoisted up masts to avoid acts of vandalism and ensure thorough watering. These poles reach the tree tops to relieve them of the salinity in the air, and provide support for the catenaries from which the lighting is hung. The masts are set out regularly in rows, marking diagonal lines across the ground plan of the park.

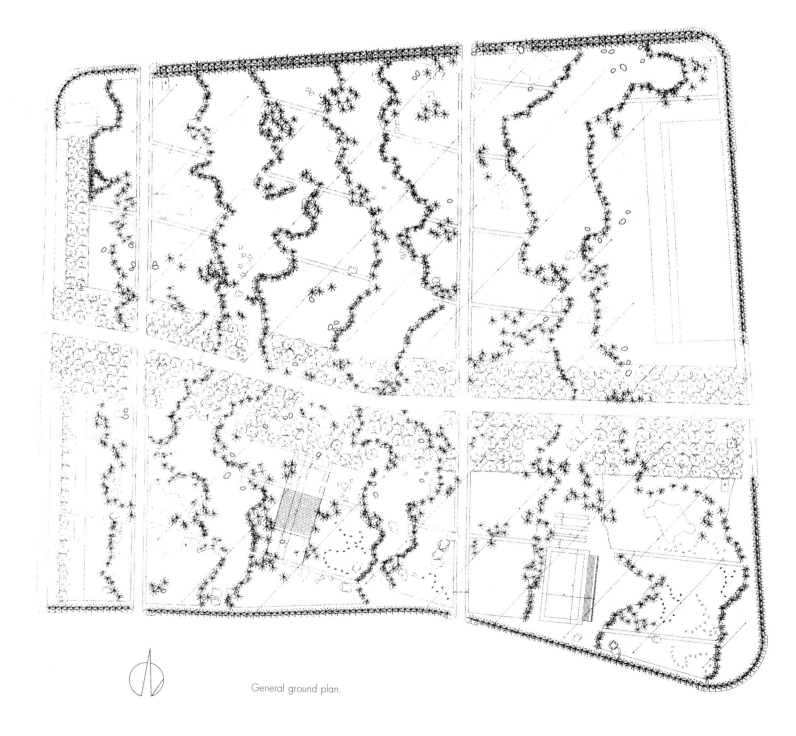

General ground plan.

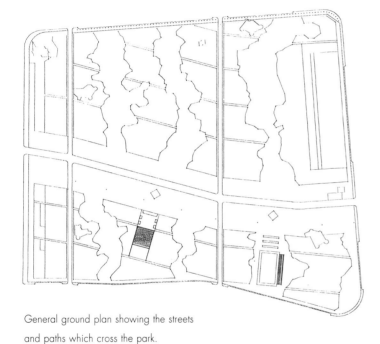

General ground plan showing the streets
and paths which cross the park.

Location: La Línea de la Concepción,
Cádiz, Spain.
Client: General Directorate of Urban Development.
Junta de Andalucía. Public Land Corp.
Collaborators: Iñaki Alday, Nuria Bordas,
Arturo Frediani, Marisa García,
Clara Jiménez, Eduard Miralles,
Joaquín Pérez, Inés Rodríguez, Quim Rosell.
Technical architects: José María Hervas,
Carlos Sánchez.
Construction company: Fomento de
Construcciones y Contratas.
Date of project: 1990-1993.
Date of construction: 1993-1995.
Photograph: Fernando Alda.

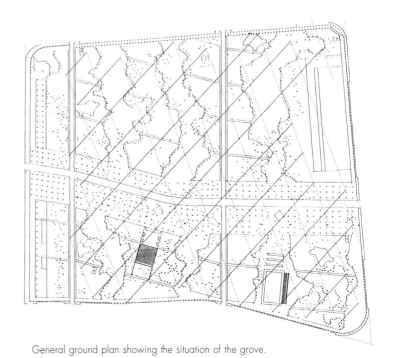

General ground plan with the diagonal lines
formed by the lighting catenaries.

General ground plan showing the situation of the grove.

In addition to one of the two open-air show areas, these photos show the park's general lighting system: the lights are suspended over the park from a series of catenaries hanging from masts which also support the sprinkler systems, adding an independent geometry to our perception of the park.

Different views of the spaces for open-air events. An abstract geometry and a green bank with tiered seating along one of its sides define the area of activity without creating hard and fast limits.

View of one of the two canopies which provide shelter for the kiosks and bars which are set up here from time to time, arranged lengthwise along the two stage constructions and next to the central avenue.

Enric Batlle & Joan Roig

River Congost Park

The story of this park is shared by many others in towns around the city of Barcelona. Here, as in other cases, the project arose from the need to develop town outskirts which were neglected during the years of uncontrolled expansion as waste land of little or no value. It is also thanks to their out-of-the-way situation that the town councils in question have been able to step in —before private initiative could intervene in search of new, unsaturated land— and create green belts for use by the whole community. The story of this park is also marked by the council's struggle to come up with the funding required to build it, which has necessarily produced a very gradual materialization phase which will stretch on until municipal resources and priorities coincide completely. Meanwhile, the passing of time may convince even the authors that certain vociferously defended initial arguments may be in need of slight alteration.

The project is centered on a 24 acre park beside the river Congost, taking the form of terraces arranged as small woods, plazas and a football ground. The course of the river from its source to its mouth was taken as the guiding thread for the creation of the different platforms.

Once the football ground had been built, the park could be used as a support for various plantations and even as a venue for Catalonia's plant-a-tree day. However, the planned structure was subject to two new conditioning factors which called for a restructuring of the proposal. Firstly the park, which originally sloped down to the river and developed in close association with it, had to take on board a new road planned to run between the two. This was incorporated into the arrangement as a new outer limit for the project.

Secondly, the football ground, which had originally been designed as an essential part of the park rather than an adjacent space, had to be separated from it: the team which played there started to move up the league, and eventually asked Batlle and Roig to design an opaque fence to redefine the formerly open pitch as now belonging to the club.

These two conditions forced the architects to come up with a new argument for the park, one which could encompass the planned uses and include what had already been built to come up with a new solution for the entire complex. This was precisely how the new structure of the park came about: irregular bushes into which a series of metal gates are set to close up the park or parts of it such as the football ground.

The park is ultimately a public space situated on the urban edge of the river Congost and bound by two courses: one on the city-side which follows the line of the existing street, the other on the river side which is a sinusoidal line. Within its boundaries, the plants are laid out in rectangular patterns in the case of the trees, or in labyrinthine enclosures in the case of the bushes, in an allusion to all the flows channeled along the river course (air, water, wind, electricity). A large sports amenity with its own entrance is located at one extreme, and is included in the park by the system already described: the bushy enclosures and metal gates which close up the football pitch, different sectors or the whole park.

In the end, arguments which were, in theory, imposed on the place and the architects led to a complete rethink, turning these incidents into the driving force of the project.

Location: River Congost, Granollers,
Barcelona, Spain.

Client: Granollers City Council.

Surface area: 24 acres.

Collaborators: Lluís Jubert, architect,

Lluís Roig, technical architect,

Teresa Galí, technical agricultural enginner.

Proyect: 1985-1996.

Works: 1986-1996.

Photographs: Teresa Galí, Eugeni Pons.

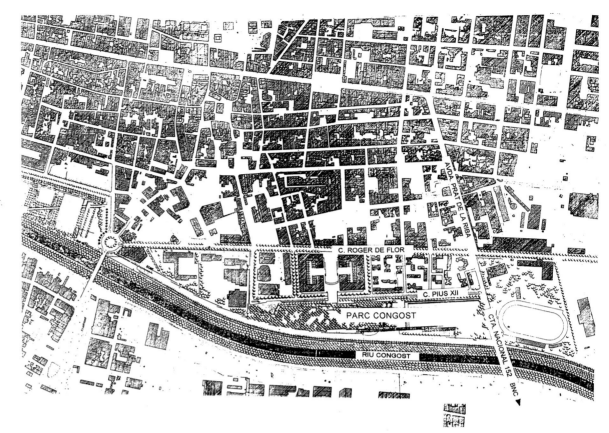

Ground plan of location.

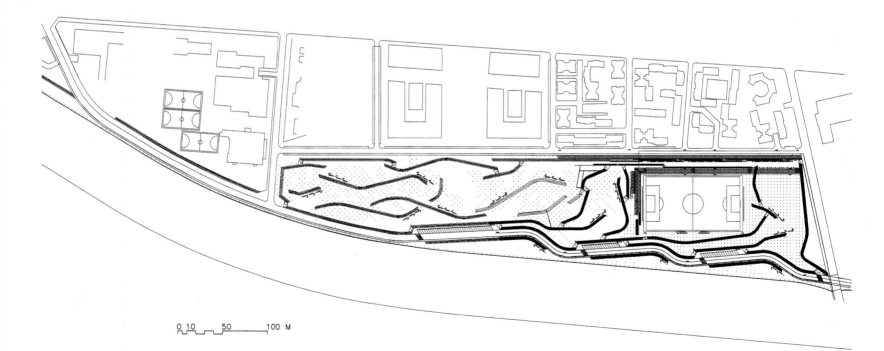

0 10   50   100 M

General ground plan.

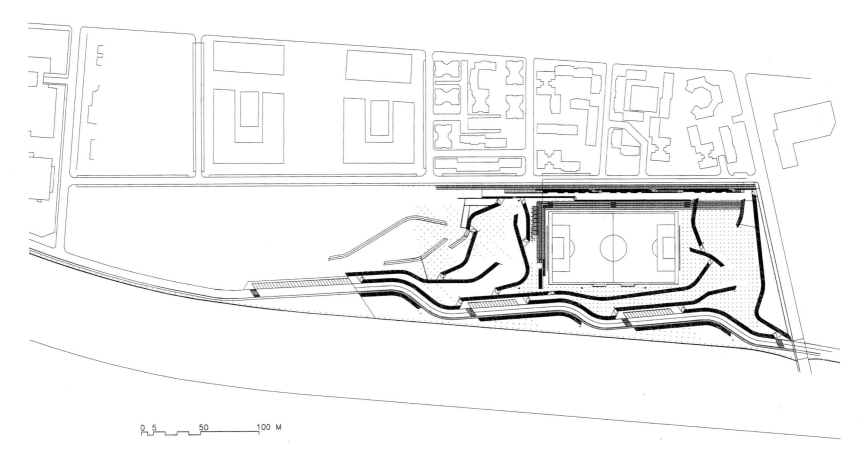

0 5   50   100 M

Ground plan of Phase 1.

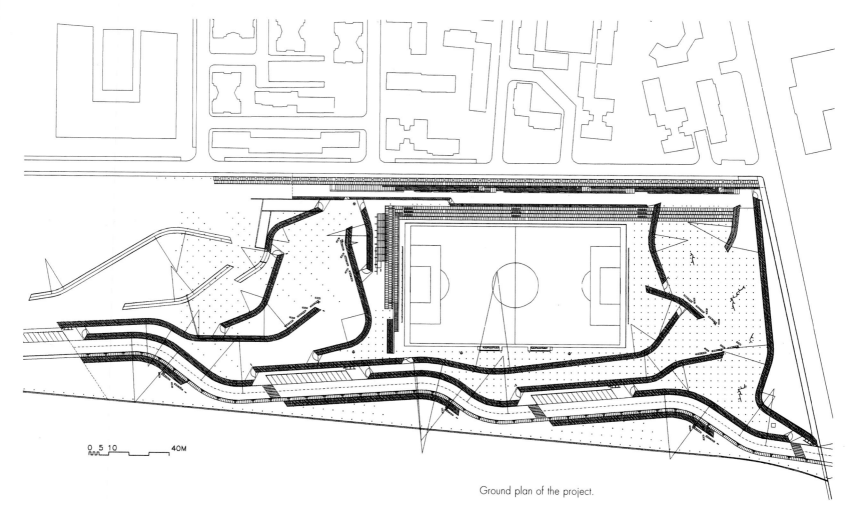

Ground plan of the project.

The metallic doors are not only the elements that close the park at night, but also the compositive element which organises the ground plan of the design and gives it its strongest image.

The pergolas, benches and lamp posts were specially designed for the park. The relationship between them is evident in both their form and the materials used.

The park is ultimately defined by a clear conceptual idea (the walls of plants and metal gates around its edges) and a series of urban furnishing designs which give the whole a unified image.

Various views and a detail of
the basic metal gate.

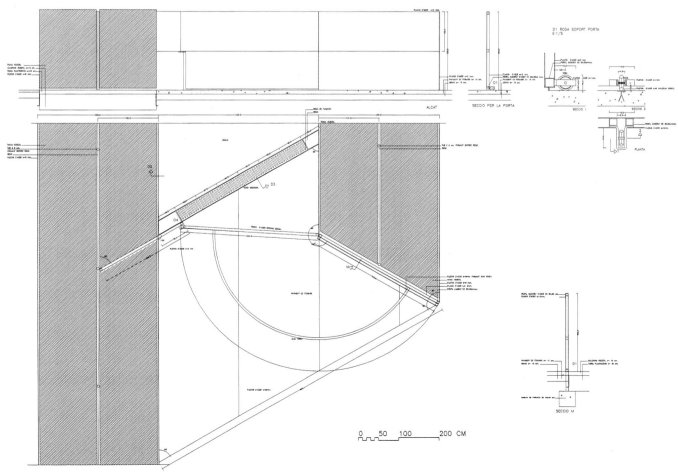

0 50 100   200 CM

Hargreaves Associates

Plan for the Guadalupe River Park

The new Guadalupe River Park runs for three miles alongside the river Guadalupe as it passes through the Californian city of San José. The sinuous course of the river, which is crossed by many bridges, is hemmed in by two important freeways, and in fact runs almost parallel to Freeway 87, connecting the center of the city with the airport. The Guadalupe had been almost forgotten by the citizens of San José, and the city authorities decided to initiate a plan for the restoration of its bed and banks, creating leisure areas and transforming the river into an element capable of articulating the center of the city and turning it into an important part of the city's image.

Hargreaves Associates, who initially acted only as consultants, ended up managing the whole park project, together with a multi-disciplinary team of hydraulic, geotechnic, environmental and civil engineers, along with 14 other associates.

The river suffered from flooding nearly every year and this was obviously one of the most important problems needing to be solved. A preliminary project carried out by the Army Engineering Corps consisted of providing the river with an adequate bed to control the periodic fluctuations in volume. The building of a concrete channel solved the problem adequately, but did nothing to improve the spatial qualities of the zone. Hargreaves Associates, conscious of the basic problem posed by the floods, adopted a design whose central point was a solution to this question.

The plan was carried out at two basic levels. Firstly, flood control was achieved by grading the section of the canal, and this necessarily conditioned the development of the rest of the park. Simultaneously, a series of open spaces were created along the river banks, articulated by the linear course of the river itself.

The varied nature of the river banks, ranging from natural riverside vegetation to areas of urban development, provided the project with a diversity of environments which could be used to blur the separation between river and city. This graduation of environments worked both ways, starting both with the river and with the city. To this end, key points situated near to the river, such as the Children's Discovery Museum, the San José Arena or the Center for Performing Arts, served to promote the public spaces surrounding them, which received a decidedly urban treatment in the form of terraces and squares which mark the course of the river as it penetrates into the city.

The longitudinal axis of the park is marked by a gradual development of space. The banks of the river narrow as it approaches the city center while in the area near the airport the river widens and flows more freely.

Near Guadalupe Gardens, winding footpaths run between plant-covered dunes by the river banks, breaking the monotony of the riverside path. A smooth slope flows down to the river to form lawns which have children's play areas and picnic facilities. Further on, as the available space lessens on the river bank, it is terraced until it reaches the point where the park bifurcates. This point has received special attention in the plan. The riverside vegetation dissolves into spaces with a more urban character which in turn connect with the freeway on one side and the San José Arena, a multipurpose center for exhibitions and shows, on the other. An information and education center has been located if at the main entrance to this area of the park. From here to the point where the two freeways cross, the park becomes more of a riverside walk, given the narrowness of the banks, although various accesses have been provided.

The virtue of this new park lies in the diversity of its spaces, ranging from the completely urban to areas almost free from development, which together form a new space which reclaims an area right in the middle of a big city and imbues it with an unusually high level of environmental quality.

Location: San José, California, U.S.A.

Client: City of San José, California.

Collaborators: AN West (engineering),

AGS (geotechnical engineering),

H.T. Harvey & Associates (ecological

and environmental planning).

Date of design: 1988.

Date of completion: 1998.

Photographs: Hargreaves Associates.

Area near the Center for Performing Arts.

Model of the area near the San José Arena.

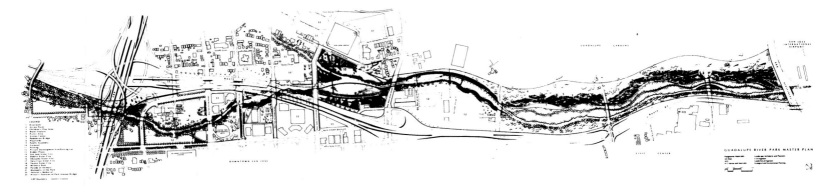

General plan of the complex in the center
of the city of San José in California.

The area around the San José Arena contains a variety of public spaces which graduate the meeting between the river and the city, blurring their limits. Moving from the paved areas through the grassy dunes and sandlots for children, the park gradually encounters the riverbank vegetation beside the water.

Area of contact with the urban center. At this point the park adopts more geometrical lines which gradually lose clarity near the river where the indigenous vegetation still conserves its more or less wild character.

Where there is not sufficient space for the section of the river bed to be smoothed out, it is terraced parallel to the grades of the riverside path that runs throughout the park.

BU
AND LAN

ILDINGS
IDSCAPE

Landscape interventions on and around public buildings always have two requirements to meet: first of all, they are an announcement, a distinctive sign which gives character to the immediate surroundings and makes the building in question almost instantly recognizable. Secondly, they aim to point up the architectural space in which they are situated to encourage greater use and make them more pleasant to be in, even though they are, in most cases, purely visual.

The projects presented under this heading are not designed for intensive use, as in most cases they are meant to be seen rather than physically used. Geometrical design therefore comes into its own, taking the sophisticated form of planimetric developments which compose natural and plant elements according to an architectural order. Here, the essence and principal purpose of landscape architecture is taken to its limit: the sensitive, poetic qualities of architecture are picked up, stripped of function and distilled into places and objects with a capacity for evocation. Plant life is abstracted, taken out of context and resituated with the purpose of reproducing the exact opposite to a specific place in nature. The result is a total abstraction of the natural which purports to construct a new type of clearly artificial landscape, playing on the capacity of plants to stimulate the imagination, recalling and representing other places and sensations.

Burton Associates

South Chula Vista Library Gardens

Richard Legorreta, the architect of the South Chula Vista Library building in California, is perhaps the most prolific and internationally known contemporary Mexican architect, and one whose works express a strong sense of Mexican identity. He has received many commissions, not only from his own country, but also from the frontier states of the U.S.A., where his particularly populist vision of Mexican traditional architecture seems to fulfil the needs of the numerous community of Mexican origin, in search of the roots of their own cultural identity.

The new building has been designed with the idea of a Mexican agricultural hacienda in mind. It combines the popular and the modern, offering a new vision of indigenous architecture by means of elements such as light and climatic filters, a festive use of colour and a reworking of the spatial qualities of the patio.

The landscaping, carried out by Burton Associates in collaboration with Richard Legoreta, has followed similar guidelines. Working in tandem with the Library staff and with the community of Chula Vista, an attempt has been made to express the bi-cultural nature of the community. The design seeks to condense the different ecosystems of the region, both in the interior and the exterior of the building. The landscaping of the exterior is clearly divided into two parts. The above-ground parking lot, with its abundance of trees, emulates an area of *huertos* or market gardens, traditional in the area's agriculture. The road leading to the parking lot is lined with palm trees. The other landscaping elements which surround the building are all very close to it. A base of pebbled paving interrupted by walkways supports lone cacti and other desert species, sometimes in combination with areas planted with flowers of varied hues.

The interior patios each have a different theme. Each one contains a different type of ecosystem to respond not only to the conditions of light and space of the patio itself, but also to the specific design which is developed in the interior in an attempt to explore the sensory qualities of each element.

In the desert patio, two small groups of spiny desert plants emerge from a bed of pebbles. The composition is completed by a group of aligned prisms of an intense dark fuchsia color. The power which these elements acquire is, by itself, enough to give character to the patio. The patio is only open on one side and may be viewed serenely from a distance.

The second patio uses the same resources. The floor is covered by a single species of riverside plants. Small white flowers appear in the higher leaves. At tree-top height, a mirrored ball appears among the flowers which reflects the patio. The patio gives on to the reading rooms, and its uniformity offers a calm atmosphere to the readers.

The third patio is different, as it has access from the interior and is not designed to be viewed through glass but rather as a place for rest asit is in fact the continuation of a lounge area. Shade is provided by a brightly-colored pergola and by some small trees and the atmosphere is refreshed by the water of a pond around the edge.

In each patio specific solutions are found to the requirements of the design, which at the same time recreates a slice of typical ecosystems in an attempt to bring nature, with its archetypal images, to a public building in search of character and roots.

Site plan of the library and its garden.

Location: Orange Avenue,
Chula Vista, California, U.S.A.

Client: City of Chula Vista,
California, U.S.A.

Associates: Legorreta
Architects & L.P.A.

Date: 1995.

Photograph: Burton Associates.

The exterior of the building seeks to recreate typical regional landscapes. Whether it is the palm plantation, the market gardens or the stony desert, each actuation occupies a precise place in relation to the building.

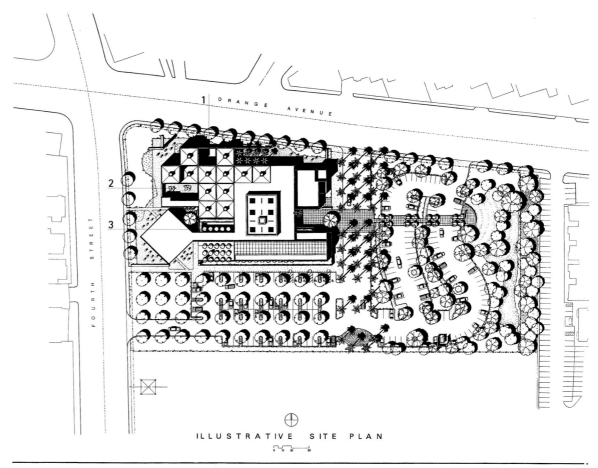

ILLUSTRATIVE SITE PLAN

SOUTH CHULA VISTA LIBRARY
CHULA VISTA, CALIFORNIA

Patio n°.1. Just one type of riverside plant occupies the entire patio. A mirrored ball appears among the flowers. The patio's calm and subdned nature aids contemplation in the library's reading room.

Above:
Patio n°.3. This patio is accessible
from the interior as it forms the
continuation of a lounge area. Filters
of light, water and shadow create an
environment conducive to relaxation.

Patio n°.2. A few elements, surrounded
by festive colours and lying on a rocky
bed, are capable of ordering
the space. The view from the interior
centers of the great force acquired
by two small groups of desert plants
and intensely colored prisms.

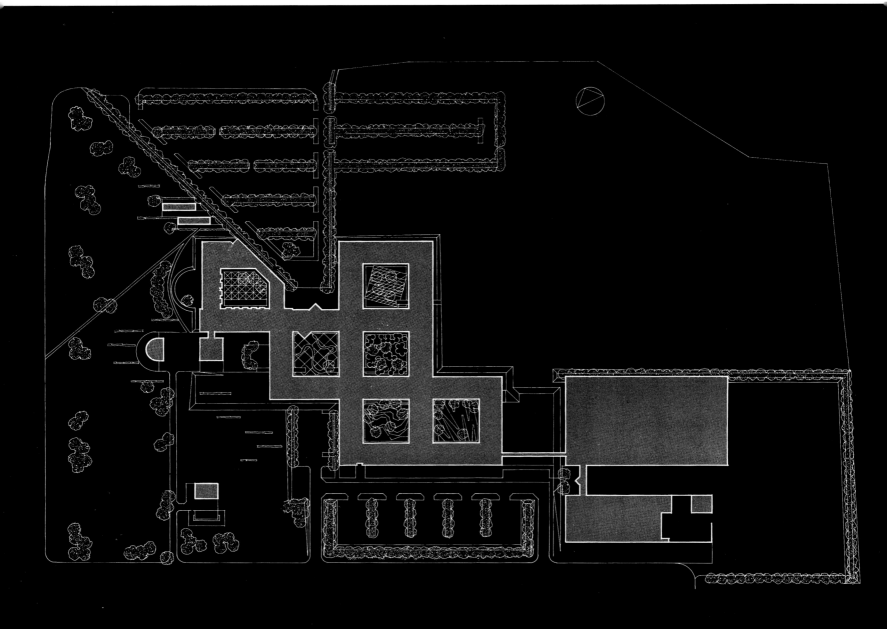

Preben Skaarup

Three Gardens in the Patios of the Telecenter Fyn Building

The Telecenter Fyn Building is organized in the form of a grid of slim shapes that leave a series of small interior patios which light and ventilate the buildings. The two-story patios are completely enclosed and have an important visual impact on the building, but were not designed for any specific use and were constructed as closed spaces. Of the six patios incorporated in the design, five form perfect squares, while the sixth has an irregular shape. Preben Skaarup was commissioned to work on three of the square patios, and his design is a landscape recreation that uses the absence of any formal design to create an experimental interplay of forms and materials.

The common denominator of the three different interventions is the complex use of the geometry of the square to create a series of developments which result in three very different configurations. Skaarup himself likens these developments to a game, with its own internal rules and movements.

In the first patio, the designer plays with the superposition of different layers in the same plane in such a way that their intersection in the final result determines the complexity of the whole. The first layer consists of a diagonal variation of the geometry of the square which signals paved borders simulating paths. The second layer is defined by a sinuous curve which gives way to a low partition. Another layer incorporates a free linear segmented geometry which is represented by metal supports for climbing plants. Each of the layers is formalized by either geometrical or mathematical laws which condition the dimensions of each element and leave little room for arbitrariness. Skaarup acknowledges the debt he owes to the procedures used by Tschumi in La Villette Park and also incorporates some of the formal and landscape criteria of his own country.

The laws governing the second patio are less numerous. The perimetral square contains a smaller square that is gyrated to leave four triangles which appear as four small ponds surrounding the central island. The island's interior geometry, with its laws of autonomous generation, defines the areas paved with stone, the grassy zones and the position of the partitions. In this design, the elements in play and the variations which they undergo are fewer and simpler.

The third patio plays with the possibilities of height to create a slope that reaches up to the second floor of the building on one side. In this way, the rules of the game coincide with the laws of an artificial terrain which creates a series of artificial terraces over which alternating grass and paved areas are also combined. Large granite balls have been placed on the slope to act as "inhabitants" of the space and form isolated landmarks in the continuous slope of the topography. Once again, the use of a few elements combined in a complex interplay creates a design whose richness in variation is due only to the stone, the grass, the partitions and little more. Skaarup exploits the geometries projected over the plane to the limit, and the sense of this procedure is further emphasized if we remember that the patios are designed to be seen from the overlooking windows of the Fyn Telecenter building, from where the geometry of the designer's empirical vision is manifest. In contrast, there is more reluctance in the use of height. The first patio presents a smooth undulating topography based on the superposition of the various layers; the second is practically flat; and the third consists of a series of slopes which are limited by the levels of the first and second floors. The primarily planimetric nature of Skaarup's landscapes is patent.

The Telecenter Fyn building is organized
as a mesh of bars, leaving six small
square patios in its interior, designed
to be inaccessible.

Location: Odense, Denmark.
Client: Fyns Telefon.
Associates: Anne Lundager, Jonna Majgaard Krarup,
Frode Birk Nielsen, Vivi Petersen.
Date of competition: 1986.
Date of design: 1986-1991.
Date of construction, first phase: 1988-1990.
Date of construction, second phase: 1991-1993.
Photographs: Preben Skaarup

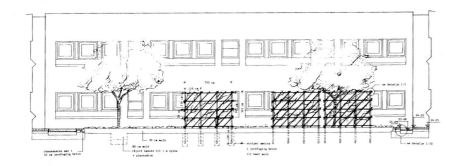

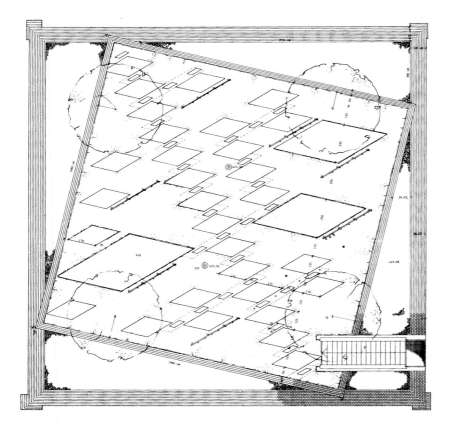

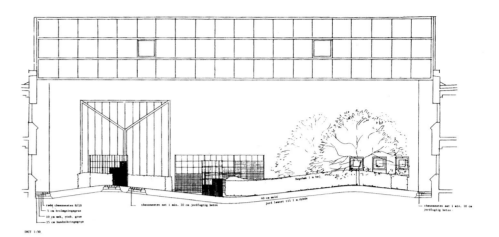

The level of geometric elaboration of each of the three designs results in a high level of sophistication, achieved with the use of few materials; stone, grass, partitions and some artificial elements which protrude above the planes.

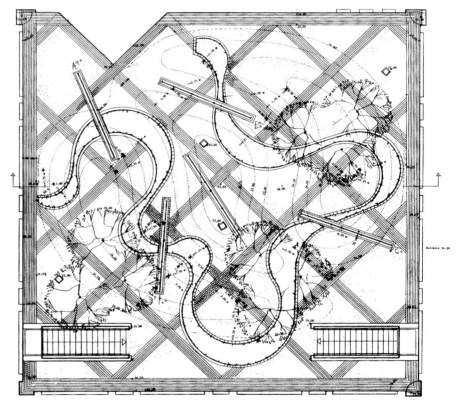

The designs can be seen as interplays
of variations on the square, with their
own internal rules and movements,
governed by geometry and leaving little
room for arbitrary decisions.

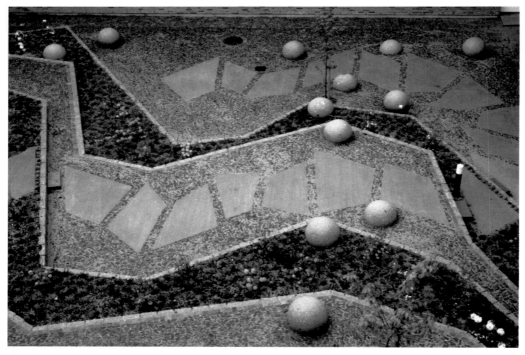

Planimetric representation plays a
determining role in the formalization of
these small gardens, which are designed
not for habitation but rather to be seen
from the windows directly above.

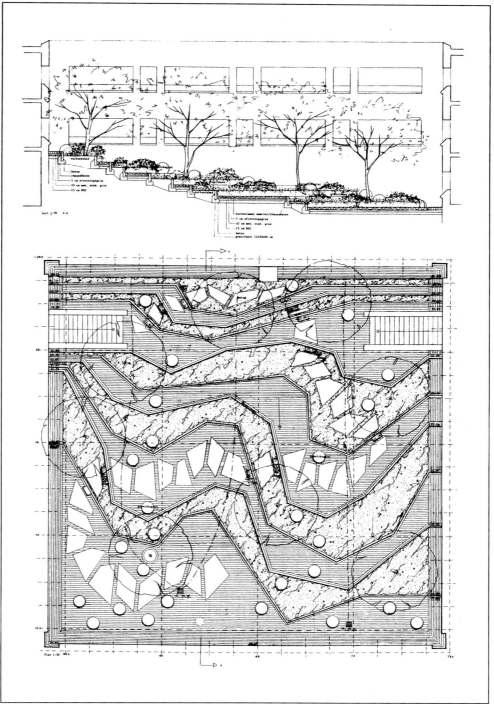

Müller-Wehberg-Knippschild i.L

Courtyards of the Ministry of Economy

After the reunification of the two Germanies, Berlin, in its role as the new capital, had to accommodate a wide range of new government services, whether in existing buildings or new constructions. The new headquarters for the Ministry of Economy reused the buildings of an old hospital complex in the city center, made up of the government hospital and a recent building. The landscape architecture team formed by C. Müller, J. Wehberg and E. Knippschild undertook the entire process of restructuring and conversion of the gardens and courtyards of the ministry's new head office.

The criteria applied for the systematization of the building's outdoor spaces were situation and relative importance within the complex. The team designed entrances, front gardens, parking areas, the main courtyards, various small courts and a few outbuildings with attached gardens. Here we show a series of gardens laid out around one of the courts; these are perhaps a particularly difficult space to resolve as a result of the special conditions of light and the ground they occupy. Here it was necessary to produce pleasant spaces for the office workers to look out into from what were rather somber courts due to the narrow section of the light wells and the impossibility of planting trees on land which comprises basement ceilings.

The six courts respond to clear-cut ideas in terms of form and plant life. The basic idea was to create miniature model ecosystems for each one. The names given to each of them reveal their contents unambiguously: stone, pool, meadow, café, water and forest. They all share a characteristic typology, the type of vegetation which a landscaped roof can support, and repeated design motifs like a cubic bench-stone which reappears and various diagonal strip designs.

Stone court. The smallest of all. A garden with no plants, like the stone gardens of Japanese inspiration. A bed of blackish stone is the background for a network of great white stones. Three steel strips, placed across the court at random, bisect odd stones they find in their path.

Marsh court. Wooden footbridges floating over a watery bed make it passable. Small patches of shingle with appropriate plant species give the final touches to the desired marshy atmosphere.

Meadow court. A striped pattern similar to the previous courts divides the surface up into different areas. The way out of the building is paved to create a doormat. The remainder is either overgrown with grass or ivy mixed with other plant species which scarcely rise above ground level. A row of small bushes runs alongside a more or less diagonal strip which marks out an axis.

Café court. A terrace leading out of the cafeteria. It is paved in stone, as though it were a plaza. A pattern of darker strips picks up the composition of the other courts. Only a round flower bed is set apart from the terrace area where the café tables are arranged. A small tree, surrounded by bushes, adds a picturesque touch to the hard marble slabs of the paving.

Water court. Here the design of the stone strips running from one edge to the other of the court includes small channels of water which form an irrigation system. The irregular areas left between the lines drawn out in this way are planted with low-level wetland plant life.

Forest court. This court is divided up into different zones for different species, which edge the court, leaving a central area which is grassed over. The two doorways leading out of the building are marked by small areas of hard paving. Red and white lacquered metal posts are arranged at random, but with the intention of marking out a loosely related group, like a real forest. Creepers grow up them in imitation of the trees which cannot be planted, due to the shallow soil on the basement roof.

The general idea of the project was to come up with a theme for each court which would allow the space to develop its own personality, different to its neighbors. The aim was to relieve the monotony of the different working spaces in their relation with the inevitable in-between spaces produced by certain types of historical building. The courts are taken as spatial escape valves that become points of reference which the building's inhabitants can physically enjoy or simply view through the windows while they work.

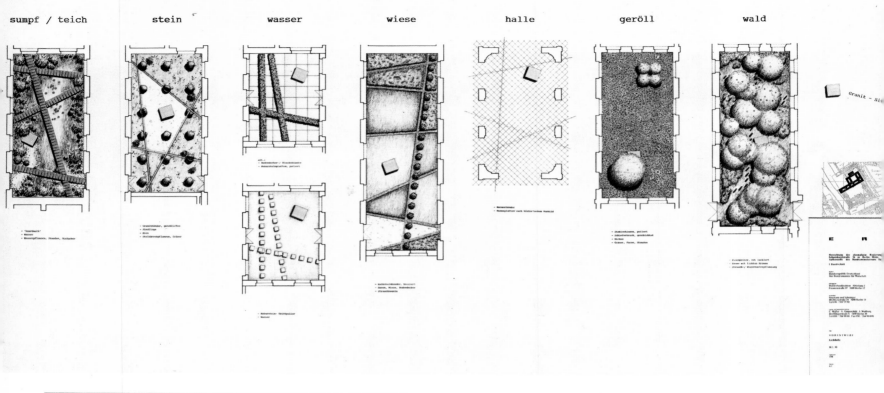

Lichthöfe

sumpf / teich	stein	wasser	wiese	halle	geröll	wald

Various ground plans of the gardens from
the preliminary design, which outlined the
idea of characterizing the courts
by model ecosystems and materials.

One of the courts prior to the design project.

Location: Ministry of Economy,

Scharnhorststrasse, 36, Berlin, Germany.

Client: The German Ministry of Economy.

Date: 1992.

Photographs: Erik-Jan Ouwerkerk and J. Wilhelm.

Marsh court.

Meadow court.

Looking upwards from the bottom
of one of the narrow light wells.

Café terrace-court.

Water court with its
preliminary diagram.

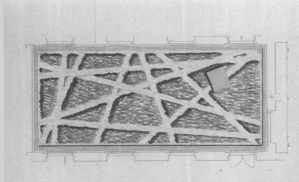

Forest court.

Preliminary diagram.

Luc Lampaert

The Concrete Garden

This project is set in a typical small, private, urban precinct: a patio-garden at the back of a house measuring 450 sq. ft. surrounded on three sides by a nine-foot-high wall. The patio is assigned the usual function of a small opening for domestic life in the outdoors. These small back yards tend to be fitted out as poor simulations of large garden spaces, with lawns, plastic chairs and table, awnings and sun umbrellas, and too many plants for such a small space. The result is more a fiction of a garden than an actual garden.

When faced with this space, Luc Lampaert decided that the tools of landscape architecture were ideal for the dimensions of the place; they could be used to create an ambience which would adapt to its function without recourse to a mockery of the inhabitant's dreams or aspirations, with allusions to wider open spaces in the form of a repertoire of figurative resources.

When he set to work, Lampaert defined the space as "hostile", basically due to the smallness of size and the impossibility of carrying out a real landscape project. His approach took the form of a series of elements loaded with a pronounced semantic charge, signs which refer us to archetypal elements from nature which, thanks to their hermeticness, are open to a variety of interpretations by visitors. These signs take very "concrete" architectural form, are few and very clear, and are capable of defining the future atmosphere of the garden all by themselves. So the ground is covered with yellow gravel, though nine small squares of grass remind us of its more normal applications in gardens. Rather than becoming a lawn in its direct, literal sense, these nine squares make indirect allusions to it. In the same way, one of the garden's corners contains nine thick tree trunks cut from the great trees in the nearby woods; the trunks stand nine feet high, like the garden wall. This creates an allusion to the trees without introducing them literally into this small area, and at the same time making the most of the full height of the patio. Another natural landscape element is introduced in the form of a small pond, out of which the trunks rise. Finally, the outer wall is crowned by a regular pattern of empty clay flowerpots, representing the semantic presence of the more domestic, workaday aspect of private gardens.

The outer wall is painted green and partially grown over with ivy, which is perhaps the only element which plays a literal role in this patio-garden. On the day of its opening, the interior designer Jeanpierre Detaeye arranged candles around the foot of the wall, and temporarily hang a projection in the form of a section of laminated metal girder to introduce some elements of domestic life more in keeping with constructed interiors.

With this approach Luc Lampaert managed to make the most of the architectural qualities of the elements he introduced to create a landscape which is really in keeping with the small scale of this little patio. The result produces a personal ambience without direct or simulated recourse to natural elements, avoiding any processes of substitution or falsification. The overall combination of signs creates a hermetic atmosphere, an almost sacralized atmosphere which appears to conceal a hidden meaning, while responding to various possible readings. But the origin of the decisions about the project lies in a clear analogy between the pieces used and the distant references to nature which are introduced metaphorically into the enclosure in a way which is very much in keeping with its specific scale. To some extent, we could say that Luc Lampaert has translated the language of nature into clearly architectural forms, taking a short cut which merely provides us with a glimpse of their relationship to the original paradisiac landscape.

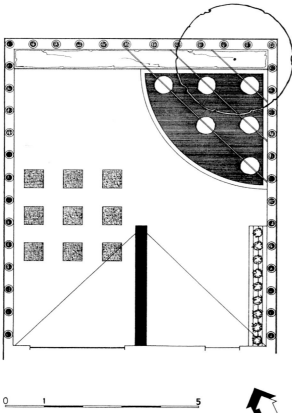

0 1   5

Location: Krommenelleboog 40,

Gent, Belgium.

Surface area: 450 sq. ft.

Collaborator: Jeanpierre Detaeye, interior designer.

Date: 1994.

Photographs: Bart Dewaele, Luc Lampaert.

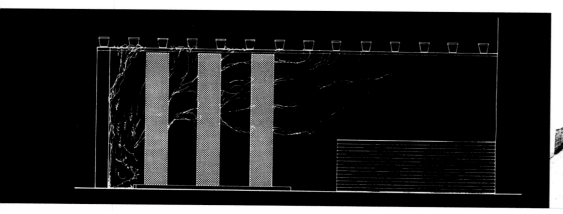

The great trunks hewn from trees in the nearby woods indirectly represent these woods inside the garden and exactly match the nine feet enclosure walls in height. Right, the empty flower pots crowning the garden wall.

The concrete garden introduces a series
of elements which are strongly marked
by their architectonic nature to adapt to
the diminutive dimensions of the garden.

The elements introduced into the garden shadow the height of the outer wall, reinforce the solid nature of the ground plan and reproduce nature's original components by metaphor and allusion.

Fumihiko Maki & Associates
Sasaki Environment Design Office
Kaze-no-Oka Crematorium

From the beginning, the construction of a new crematorium in an area of beautiful countryside on the outskirts of the Japanese city of Nakatsu was conceived as a collaborative project between a firm of architects and one of landscape architecture. This collaboration was designed to ensure that instead of both firms working separately and later uniting their work, the project would be a joint venture from the very beginning. In this way, the design possibilities would be multiplied, as the architecture of the building would become a landscape element, integrated in an overall design which consisted of the careful construction of a new landscape.

The crematorium building itself consists of a one-story edifice characterized by its horizontality, whose profile, which is visible from the park, becomes one of the principal elements of the new landscape. The profile consists of three main parts: the inclined volume of the chapel (the highest point of the complex); a blind, sloping crowning wall which encloses some of the functional areas of the crematorium; and a porch which both separates and unites the other two elements. Behind this screen, the design of the crematorium proper occupies a generous space and is scrupulously organized according to the functional requirements of funeral rites. However, even the organization of the interior forms a precise kind of landscape: by strict control of the light allowed in, of the pattern of patios, of the ponds, the openings and the screens, a walk through the interior acquires all the qualities of a landscape experience. In this way, the interior too becomes a part of the park, which is not simply limited to the planted areas but embraces the entire site.

In contrast, the green areas of the park receive a treatment with clearly architectural connotations, with a distinct center being created in the form of an elliptic area which sinks into the ground as one approaches. The form of the ellipse overlaps the layout of the crematorium building, suggesting an interwoven geometric system, the third part of which is composed of a series of ancient sepulchers that were discovered before the project commenced, and which, although occupying a separate area, also interweave with the ellipse and thus with the overall design.

Architectural methods and landscape instruments are mixed and combined throughout the site meaning that the architecture becomes a mechanism for the construction of a landscape, while the landscape constantly resorts to architectural mechanisms. The design of the park makes clever use of changes in the paving, isolated elements such as the trees, extremely rigid geometric topographical patterns, etc. The idea of vertical movement is ever-present: in the building this is conveyed by the openings, and in the park by the rises and falls in level which culminate in the low point in the middle of the ellipse, which seems to draw together all the elements. The inclined volume of the chapel appears to question this fundamental feeling of verticality in an apparent renunciation of the most intrinsic qualities of architecture.

While the various routes through the park are organized with a planimetric abstraction which is never sufficient to determine the nature of the project, the real point of view at which the design is aimed is the horizontal vision of the spectator. Even the crematorium building seems to have been designed as an elevation. There is a total emphasis on the views generated by the design, with objects such as the building, the trees and the walls repeatedly emerging from behind a grade, and other objects being hidden behind a smoothly inclining slope. The authentic plane of the design is the elevation and the numerous sections, which assume the traditional role of the ground plan. The same happens in the interior of the crematorium: the height of the openings, the spaces and the wall panels exploit all the possibilities offered by the vertical dimension. The landscaping of the site appears to have been carried out not only for, but also from, an empirical viewpoint, and the vision of the spectator plays the role of connecting it with the spiritual dimensions of the place and with its ultimate purpose of accommodating death and the feelings it generates.

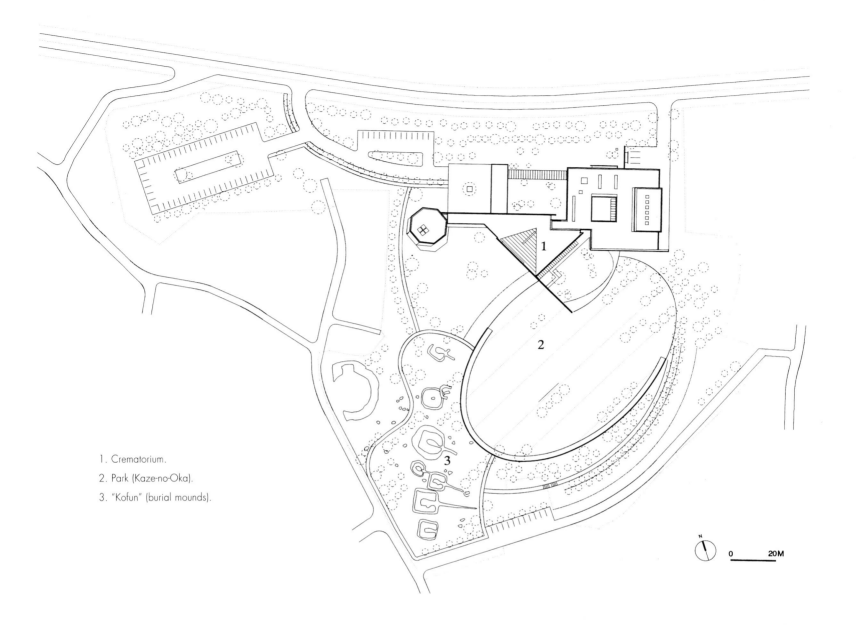

1. Crematorium.
2. Park (Kaze-no-Oka).
3. "Kofun" (burial mounds).

Location: Nakatsu, Japan.

Client: Nakatsu City Council.

Surface area of park: 35,862 sq. ft.

Date of design: 1993-1994.

Date of construction: 1995-1997.

Photographs: Nácasa & Partners inc.

The silhouette of the crematorium
building, seen from the park, is one of
the deliberately placed elements which
make up the overall landscape.

The landscape design repeatedly uses
the device of making the elements
appear from behind a grade. This sites
the spectator in a specific place,
generates depth and above all, avoids
the possibility of the landscape being
seen as one undifferentiated whole.

0   10M

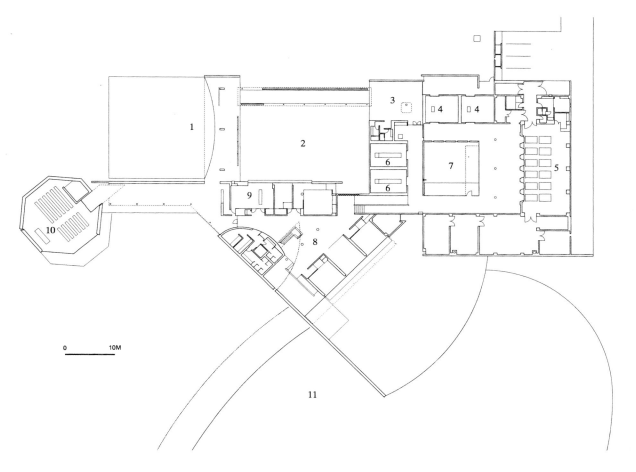

1. Parking lot.
2. Patio.
3. Entrance porch.
4. Oratory.
5. Crematorium.
6. Vigil chapel.
7. Patio.
8. Waiting room.
9. Offices.
10. Chapel.
11. Park.

The interior of the crematorium is in itself a landscape formed by specific interconnected. The discrimination of the different components (the presence of the sky, the water or the panels) allows the landscape to be defined using architectural tools.

LAN OF RECR

DSCAPE
REATION

Our consumer society, as it seeks to extend the "good life", has produced social and economic structures of a new phenomenon called "leisure time". This in turn has given rise to a demand for new spaces for the enjoyment of this leisure time, involving aspects used to be incidental but now redefine the quality of the spaces and their relationship with their surroundings. The enormous cultural and sports centers of our society are used by ever more people who demand increased standards of comfort and services, while the buildings themselves are becoming so huge that their relationship with the surroundings has to be re-examined.

Leisure consumers want to be surrounded by structures and installations which respect the environment, either by means of a controlled landscape which interferes minimally with the ecosystem, or by improved control of waste, or by the quality and impact of the design. Today, it is not a simple matter of playing sport or seeking some kind of individual tourism. The visitor demands that these huge but necessary buildings should not violate the landscape, and that the minimum of resources should lessen the effect on the environment.

Designers are well aware of the situation and have become more sensitive to the surroundings of their new buildings, and their operations are no longer always mimetic. There is a desire to incorporate the new project into the existing landscape, to make it emerge from the limits between the intervention and its surroundings. Once these limits are established, the confidence given by working in the interior gives rise to actions based on the proximity or distance from these same limits, ranging from the purely artificial to the "natural" or, as it may be, the urban. The relationship between "inside" and "outside" is the grounds for buildings that respond positively not only to the surroundings but also to environmental demands.

Desmond Muirhead

Wakagi Golf Club

The design of a golf course, even taking into account the conditions imposed by the game's rules of play, is a rich opportunity for the creation of a new landscape, something unthinkable in other sporting installations. A new landscape appears, necessarily built around the fairways and greens of the different holes, that is imposed on the existing landscape which is usually rural or agricultural. Even so, the landscaping of golf courses usually adheres to a fairly standard pattern which follows the English tradition and, with little variation, repeats a series of designs which time and custom have consolidated as the prototype to follow. The various elements follow pre-established guidelines which leave little freedom of action for the designer.

Desmond Muirhead has been designing golf courses all over the world for many years now. He began the search for a language which is capable of updating the tradition of a formal approach which is anchored in a series of supposedly untouchable stereotypes. Without departing from the rigorous approach that is necessary to ensure the design satisfies all the specific requirements of the sport, there is a strong sense of innovation in these new landscapes. New ideas from outside the field of sport, linked with the place where the landscape is sited, breathe new life into the best of the English landscape tradition. In the case of the Wakagi Golf Course, it is the agricultural methods and traditions of the Saga Plain which are the key to understanding and interpreting the new design. The landscape of the Saga Plain is a floodplain which leaves little islands of cultivation, connected by narrow paths. This area of islands chained together, floating among lakes, has served as the direct inspiration for the new golf course.

The construction of the golf course, which occupies more than 11 million square feet, has been an enormous feat, moving more than 70 million cubic feet of earth, and has meant levelling slopes of more than 90 feet and filling cavities of the same depth. To obtain the apparently smooth profiles which are so well integrated into the landscape, a laborious job of adapting the land to the necessities of a golf course has been necessary. The final result seems to hide all this effort and the holes of the course are laid out effortlessly among the great masses of trees that dot the landscape.

The layout of the course imitates the agricultural pattern of the Saga Plain, with islands being linked by bridges. The player's ball soars from island to island as it approaches the hole. This chain effect is also reproduced in the general layout of the course, where the clearings in the woodland that each hole forms are linked, with their starting and finishing point being the clubhouse. The spectacular surrounding landscape frames these routes as they wind between woods, lakes and meadows, in an intelligent confluence of the English garden landscape tradition and the timeless Japanese countryside.

Special care has been taken to enrich the routes actually followed by the golfers. Copses of trees surround tiny valleys, dunes cluster round the greens and new areas of trees have been strategically placed. The various profiles presented by the great extensions of grass have merited exceptional attention, with small promontories, bunkers of various sizes and tongues of green grass protruding into the water. The course is the result of a profound study of the characteristics of the place itself, effortlessly combined with the technical requirements of the sport for which it is designed.

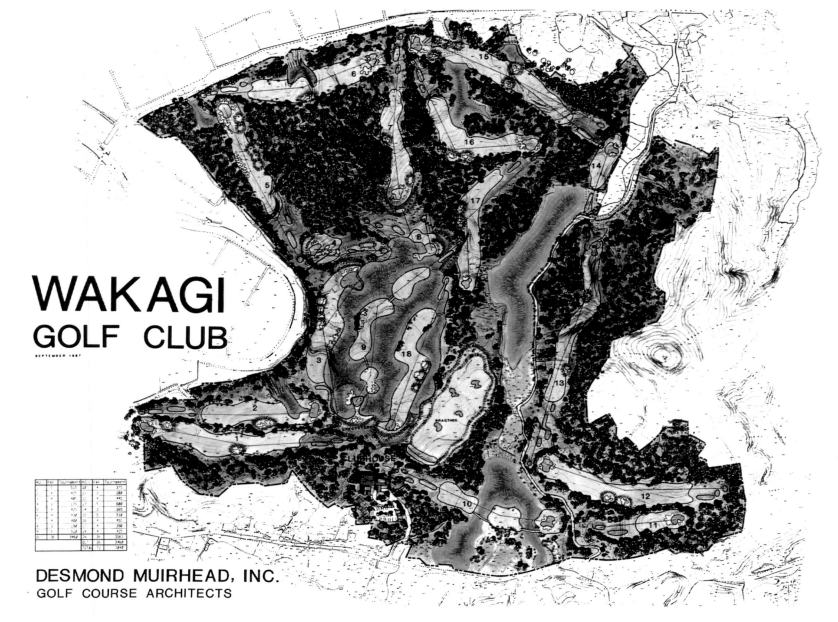

WAKAGI
GOLF CLUB
SEPTEMBER 1987

DESMOND MUIRHEAD, INC.
GOLF COURSE ARCHITECTS

General plan.

Agricultural holdings in the Saga Plain in Japan, which served as the direct inspiration of the course's design.

Location: Wakagi, Kyushu, Japan.

Client: Saison Group.

Surface area: 257 acres.

Date of design: 1988.

Date of completion: 1991.

Photographs: Paul Barton.

Views of holes 9 and 18,
looking towards the clubhouse.

Hole 9.

Hole 13.

Hole 14.

Hole 15.

Hole 17.

Hole 18.

Double page and overleaf:

Working diagrams and outlines of the course's 18 holes.

Detailed working sketches of the different parts of the course.

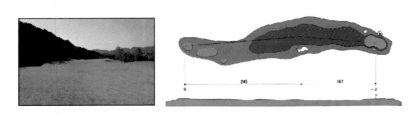

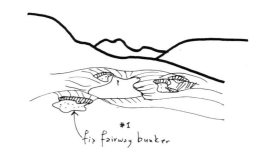

Hole 1.

Hole 2.

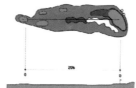

Hole 3.

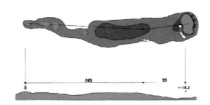

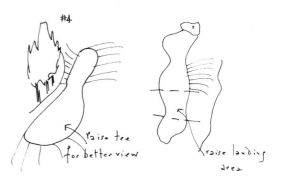

Hole 4.

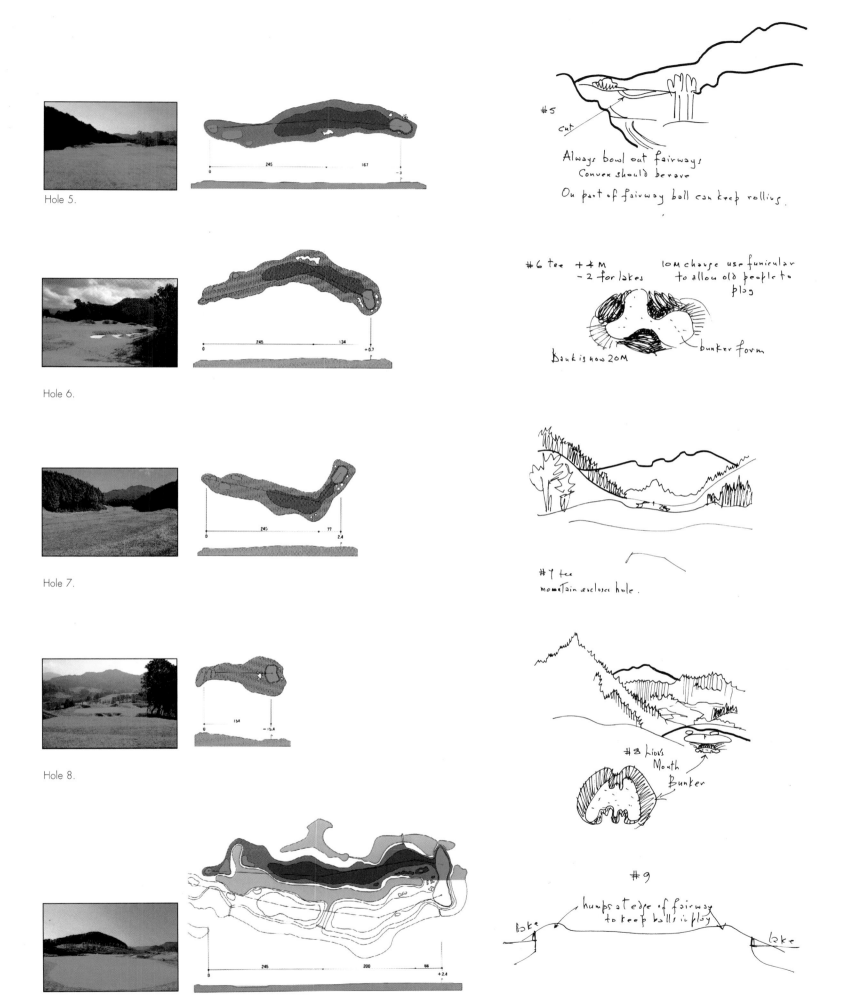

Hole 5.

Hole 6.

Hole 7.

Hole 8.

Hole 9.

#5
cut

Always bowl out fairways
Convex should be save

On part of fairway ball can keep rolling.

#6 tee + 4 M   10M change use funicular
- 2 for lakes   to allow old people to
                                    play

bunker form

Bank is now 20M

#7 tee
mountain encloses hole.

#8 Lion's
Mouth
Bunker

#9

humps at edge of fairway
to keep balls in play

lake   lake

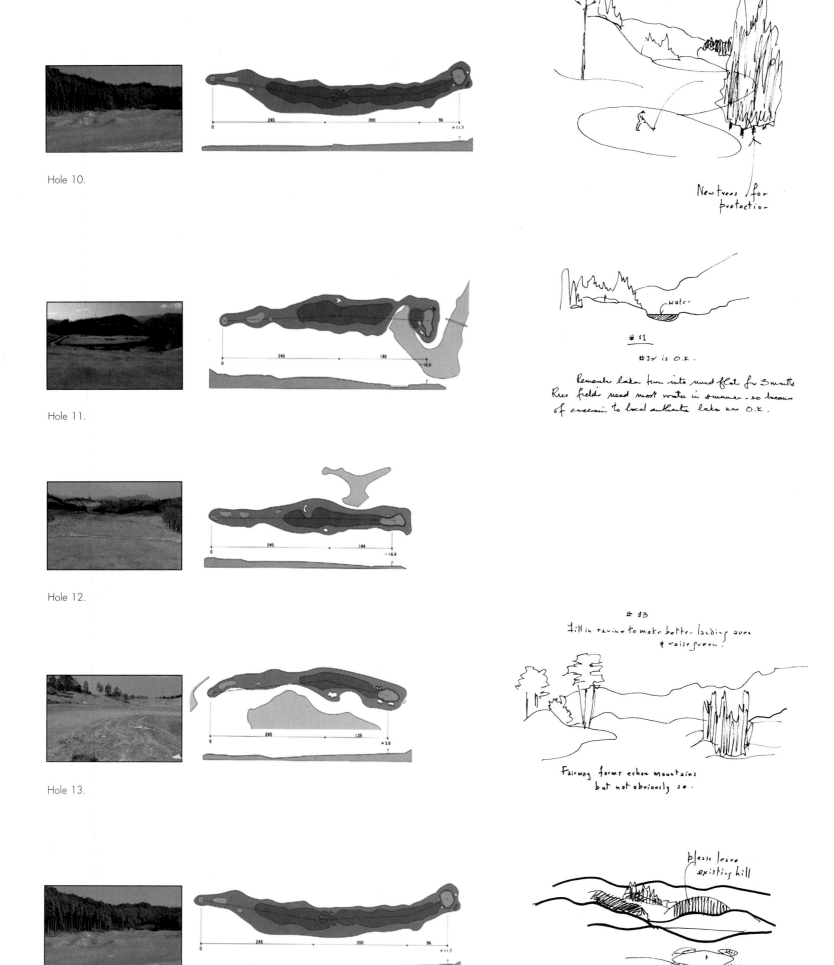

Hole 10.

Hole 11.

Hole 12.

Hole 13.

Hole 14.

 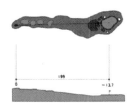 

Hole 15.

 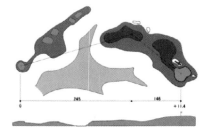 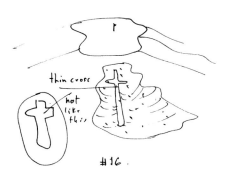

Hole 16.

 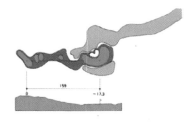 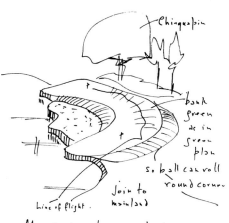

Hole 17.

 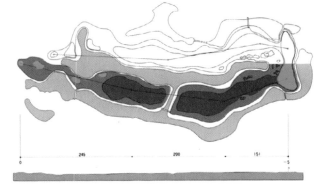

Hole 18.

Desmond Muirhead

Fuji Chuo Golf Club

A project for a golf course has to cover very diverse aspects, such as smooth functioning from a point of view of the sport, landscaping concerns in relation to the setting and the climatic aspects of the micro-climate in question. In this case, Desmond Muirhead has brought a large dose of creativity to the structure by designing the series of holes according to thematic points; this is a solution which takes in all the other aspects, as well as introducing a poetic interpretation which is imbued with respect for the proximity of its imposing neighbor, Mount Fuji.

Muirhead took the wood engravings by Japanese artist Hokusai as the basis for his organization of the course's eighteen holes. These engravings comprise 100 different interpretations of Mount Fuji, the most famous one being "The Great Wave", which is referred to at hole 17. Each of the eighteen holes was assigned a Hokusai engraving, with its own name and thematic field. Muirhead designed each hole individually around its own theme, to which he gave form by means of characteristic golfing elements: bunkers, lakes, clumps of trees, slopes, topographic control, and so on. From the point of view of landscape, the Fuji Chuo Golf Course is a splendid base which "serves" and is at all times subject to the imposing presence of Fuji as it presides over the whole course and imposes its authority all the way round the 18 holes. The landscape's many changes in the course of the day and the seasons (changes of light, presence or absence of snow, fog or other elements which alter the appearance of the mountain) are taken into account in Muirhead's project as factors of a landscape in metamorphosis, constantly changing to reflect the passage of time and the special feeling of each hour and each time of year in its atmosphere.

The design of each hole called for a basic conceptual sketch by Muirhead, covering all aspects: the presence of the volcano, the regulatory conception of the hole and therefore its topographical strategy, the reference to Hokusai's engravings and even, on occasion, an explicit reference to his person; hole 16 is one such case, a homage to the swastika which Hokusai used as a personal emblem towards the end of his life, representing the Buddhist good luck symbol which it was long before it was adopted by the Nazis. Then hole 17 is broad and shallow, with Hokusai's famous wave crossing through it.

Muirhead uses a broad repertoire of symbols from beyond the golfing world to shape such elements as went into the landscape; the resulting narration alludes to the optimum practice of this sport as well as a series of themes taken from Japanese tradition, particularly in relation to the mythical, quasi-sacred Mount Fuji which presides over the complex.

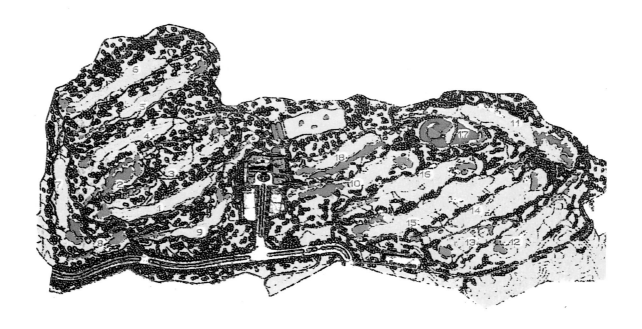

Fuji Chuo Golf Club is laid out around 18 holes, each of which refers to a specific theme of the book by Japanese artist Hokusai, *One hundred views of Fuji*. The design of each hole formally develops its given theme.

Location: Mount Fuji, Japan.
Client: Golden Ring Club Co., Ltd.
Total length of the course: 7,143 yards.
Project starting date: 1990.
Completion date: 1995.

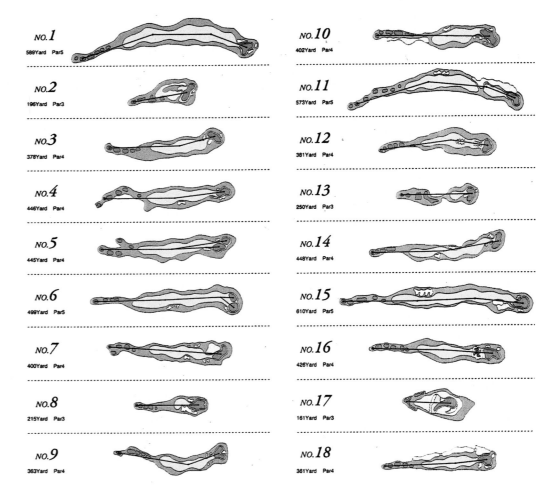

NO.1 — 589Yard Par5
NO.2 — 196Yard Par3
NO.3 — 378Yard Par4
NO.4 — 446Yard Par4
NO.5 — 445Yard Par4
NO.6 — 499Yard Par5
NO.7 — 400Yard Par4
NO.8 — 215Yard Par3
NO.9 — 363Yard Par4
NO.10 — 402Yard Par4
NO.11 — 573Yard Par5
NO.12 — 381Yard Par4
NO.13 — 250Yard Par3
NO.14 — 448Yard Par4
NO.15 — 610Yard Par5
NO.16 — 426Yard Par4
NO.17 — 161Yard Par3
NO.18 — 361Yard Par4

Hole # 1 Tea Gardens
Fuji Chuo Golf Club

Hole 1. Katakura Tea Gardens
· 589 yards · 5 Par.

Hole 2. Longevity of Hokusai
· 196 yards · 3 Par.

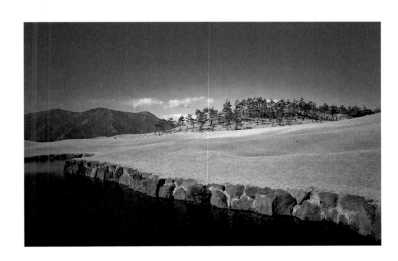

Hole # 2 Longevity
Fuji Chuo Golf Club.

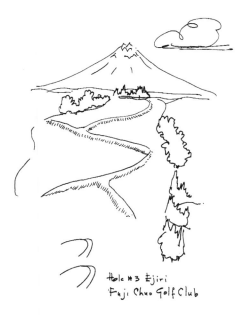

Hole 3. Ejiri-Tagonoura
- 378 yards - 4 Par.

Hole 4. Straightaway Breather
- 446 yards - 4 Par.

Hole 5. Hodogaya
- 445 yards - 4 Par.

Hole 6. Aoyama-Enza Pine
- 499 yards - 5 Par.

Hole 7. Undulating Fuji
- 400 yards - 4 Par.

Hole 9. Minobu River
- 363 yards - 4 Par.

Hole #10 Tatekawa
Fuji Chuo Golf Club

Hole 10. Honjo-Tatekawa Lumberyard
- 402 yards - 4 Par.

Hole 11. Lake Suwa -
573 yards - 5 Par.

Hole 13. Honganji Temple
- 250 yards - 3 Par.

Hole #12
Fuji Chuo

Hole 12. Enoshima
- 381 yards - 4 Par.

Hole 14. Goten-yama & Cherry Blossoms
- 448 yards - 4 Par.

Hole 16. Retirement (swastika trap)
- 426 yards - 4 Par.

Hole # 15 Waves at Kanaya
Fuji Chuo Golf Club

Hole 15. Waves at Kanaya
- 610 yards - 5 Par.

#16 Swastika Hole
Fuji Chuo

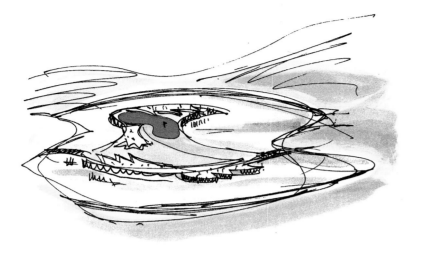

This hole, which corresponds to Hokusai's most famous engraving, The Great Wave, is broad and shallow, with the wave from the engraving crossing it diagonally in the form of a paved area with a crest-shaped edge.

Hole 17. The Great Wave
- 161 yards - 3 Par.

Hole 18. Noborito Cliffs
- 361 yards - 4 Par.

The Golf Club complex is designed as a flat base at the foot of Mount Fuji which presides over everything with its imposing presence. The modifications introduced by the change of season or climatic variations have been taken into account in the design.

Enric Batlle & Joan Roig

Manliu Mountain Area

The project was designed around an existing mountain refuge situated at over 6,000 feet in the Catalan Pyrenees, next to a dammed lake occupying a glacial hollow which lies just on the limits of the sub-alpine woods and the beginning of the true alpine vegetation.

The objective was to organize the routing of a mountain track which leads to the refuge in such a way that visitors could be informed and channeled at the same time. The main problem was combining the needs of the farmers who use the zone for their free-roaming herds of stock with a rising tide of people attracted by the natural beauty of the area. The basic requirements were a limitation of motorized traffic to avoid it spilling over onto the adjacent pastures and the provision of basic services for visitors, such as toilets, garbage collection points, a fountain and tables and barbecues for cooking. Previously, these elements had been arranged in an almost spontaneous manner.

Given the nature of the site and the objectives of the project, it was decided that stone should be used throughout, as virtually all the elements could be constructed using this material. The few existing buildings in the zone were all of stone, and in addition the material was freely available, meaning that from both an aesthetic and practical point of view it was the ideal choice. The result was that the toilets, tables, barbecues, fountains, the borders of the zone and elements for signposting and channeling traffic possess a unified appearance that is also characteristic of the area.

Using some natural dips in the terrain, a stone wall was built that folds round to form a traffic barrier. This wall contains fountains, barbecues, waste receptacles and public toilets, to act as a small service building without appearing to be any such thing. Some of the existing stones have been regrouped to form an encircling loop which subtly indicates the path to and limits of the parking area. The wall, although low, is sufficient to hide the cars parked behind it, and from the other side, mixing with the rocks strewn about the ground, appears like the ruined remains of a fictitious building.

From here the view opens onto the pastures and clumps of conifers that dot the landscape. Only a border fence of stone posts linked by wires, forming a perfect circle on the ground, limits the movements of the free-ranging animals. The fence runs over the uneven terrain between rocks and trees and is interrupted only when it reaches the lake. This action of drawing a perfect circle over the ground stands out, precisely because the rest of the intervention is intent on lying low on the ground and mimicking its surroundings. What is theoretically a fence to keep animals out becomes the element that defines the limits, physical and otherwise, of the actuation, differentiating it from the rest of the mountain. Although it seems that nothing is changed, the creation of a "place" is determined by this distinction between what is inside and outside the circle. Neither the geography nor the vegetation impede the progress of an element that is oblivious to what surrounds it. The circle establishes its position as the limit of the intervention, from which the paths to the surrounding lakes and summits depart.

Plan of the area before the intervention.

General ground plan of the design.

Location: Manliu, Meranges,
La Cerdanya, Spain.
Client: Consell Comarcal de la
Cerdanya and Generalitat de Catalunya
(Autonomous Government).
Associate: David Closas.
Date of design: 1991.
Date of construction: 1994.
Photographs: David Closas,
Gregori Civera, Enric Battle.

The wall folds back to avoid a change
in ground level, adapting and
molding itself to the terrain. Its principle
function is to contain various small
service elements, thus converting it into
a small building, but its appearance is
more that of a ruin in the middle of the
mountain landscape.

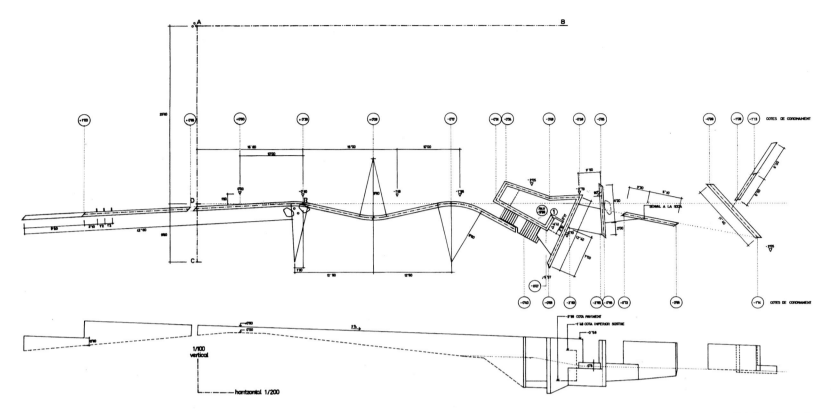

Details of the wall.

The design concentrates all the functions in the wall, which together with the perfect circle formed by the fence posts imposes its geometry on the surrounding nature without violating it. The order thus established is imposed on the broken terrain and succeeds in giving form to the area.

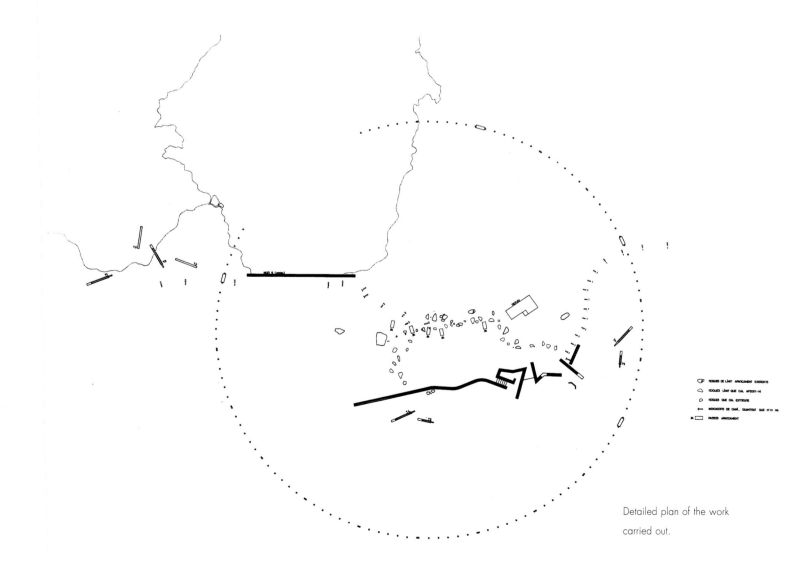

Detailed plan of the work
carried out.

The fence of stone posts and wires looks much like the area's other fencing to control stock. Only the abstract path it traces provides a clue to its cultural decontextualization. It has absolutely nothing to do with the area. It avoids all type of obstacles, confident of its own path. In this way it clearly presents what has been imposed on the landscape, marking the boundaries and leaving clear directions for the visitor.

Eduard Bru/OAS

Zoological Park

The first idea was to leave the animals practically free, letting them run around below ground, emerging at a given point so they could be seen and then disappearing again. However this idea did not work.

We then had to try to bring the usual formula up to date, although I didn't want to simulate a natural environment. Just as in some oriental palaces, it is the beasts who are invited into man's house, each construction represents the meeting of what is human and its appropriation by the animals.

The scientific project grouped the animals of the new zoo in four sectors, which were sited in an ascending sequence from the front area running parallel to the river up to the slopes which surround the site. The most valuable parts of the existing garden, such as the central axial space which housed the small zoo, were to be saved.

We made the preliminary general design, which is not shown here in detail. Detailed plans were made of the Large Bird Enclosure (a cloud of concrete, anchored to the earth by pillars of wood and metal); the Chimpanzee House (an area free from an imposed horizontal floor, with children's games on a larger scale, separated by a sliver of water, for these animals with 98% human chromosomes); the Otter Enclosure (a giant glass stairway, flooded with water which converts it into a cascade which can be climbed); and the Hippopotamus enclosure (a large pond designed to be shared).

What was actually built were the main entrance and the atrium which forms the Mandrill Enclosure. This latter had to be an open-air space, but one that was enclosed on all sides, given the nature of the animals. The enclosure also had to include an indoor sleeping space, facilities for preparing food and caring for sick animals and an area for the public that would make watching the animals easy, comfortable and interesting. For the non-expert visitor, it is precisely the observation of the games and movements of the animals throughout the whole of their space which is most attractive, so it was vitally important to provide vertical elements which encouraged movements in all directions. We built a forest of pillars which is halfway between a human architectural construction and a natural forest.

The main entrance had to be monumental, given its position —next to the river, and forming a sequence which goes Mezquita-Alcázar-Zoo— and what it represents as a leisure facility. The idea was to construct something on a large scale which would define the urban nature of the street, with special emphasis on the entrances to the Zoo and Botanical Gardens, thereby accentuating the fact that they are important urban amenities. The stepped profile seeks a transition between the scale of the street and the facade of the Gardens and the interior scale of the Zoo itself. The interior side of the profile is lowered and coincides with the roof of the Mandrill Enclosure, which is placed next to the entrance, mainly because of its popularity with visitors. The other side of the profile seeks to project the Zoo towards the street, the Botanical Gardens and the nearby river banks. The aim was to achieve a weighty presence which would form part of the much discussed but sadly unrealized plan to remodel the riverfront, a plan which included the restoration of the magnificent water-mills, the rehabilitation of the San Matías district, and new river bank developments.

Now none of this plan exists. Indeed, it is even doubtful if the plan for the Zoo will continue.

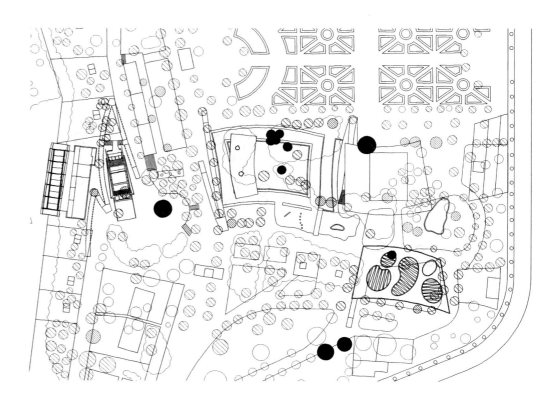

The stepped plane of the entrance forms a transition between the scale of the river and the interior of the Zoo. The lighting was designed to be emphatic so as to accentuate the presence of the Zoo in the city of Cordoba, rising above the water of the river.

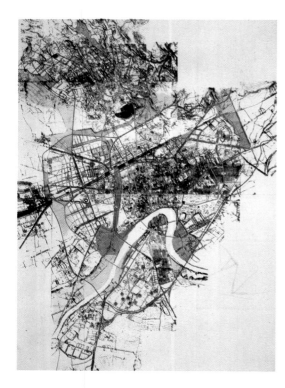

Location. Cordoba city.

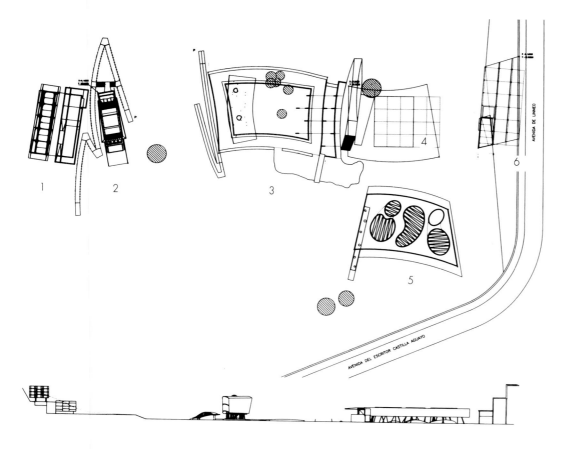

1. Hippopotamus enclosure.
2. Otter and Coypu enclosure.
3. Chimpanzee house.
4. Mandrill enclosure (first phase).
5. Exotic Bird enclosure.
6. Entrance canopy (first phase).

Location: Cordoba, Spain.

Client: Cordoba City Council.

Architects: Eduard Bru, Jaume Arbona, Antoni Balagué.

Associated architects: C. Lay, A. Arbona, A. Alcalá, A. García del Blanco, N. Lacomba, M. Raventós, A. Civit, M. Amat.

Structures: Robert Brufau.

Date of design: 1991.

Date of construction: 1993.

Photographs: Jordi Bernadó.

Mandrill enclosure. First phase.
The great roof, supported by a
metal structure which is in turn
united to the wooden poles, is
perforated many times at the
center and substituted by the
same grillwork used to finish
the vertical walls.
This is not now the ceiling of a
cage, but rather of a space.
The terrain, covered by grass,
includes an area with sufficient
water for the habitat of the
animals that occupy it.

Above:

Mandrill enclosure. First phase.

Chimpanzee house. Second phase.

Ground plans, elevation and cross sections.

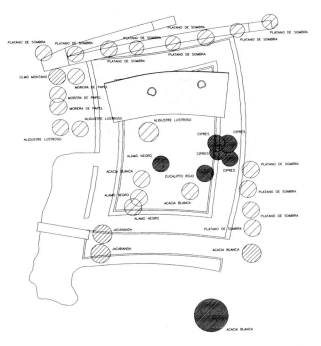

Trees affected in second phase.

Chimpanzee installations.

Trees to be conserved:

12 Plane trees.

  1 Elm.

  3 Paper mulberries.

  3 Japanese privets.

  4 Cypresses.

  3 Black poplars.

  1 Red gum.

  3 Common locusts.

  2 Jacarandas.

Trees to be transplanted:

  1 White mulberry.

  2 Elms.

  1 Common locust.

  5 Bottle trees.

  2 Japanese privets.

  2 Plane trees.

Trees to be eliminated:

  1 Common locust.

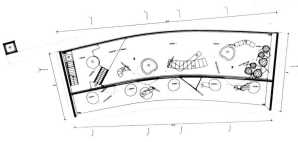

Second floor, sleeping quarters.

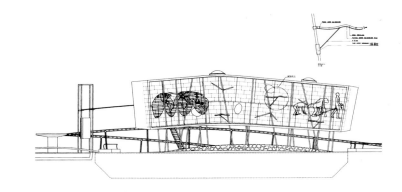

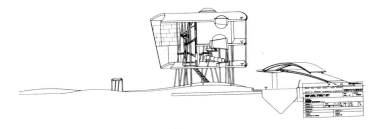

CIVIL EI
AND RECLA

IGINEERING
MING LAND

It is almost impossible to think of a natural environment in our civilization which has not undergone some form of intervention at the hands of man in terms of regional infrastructure: roads, highways, bridges, dams, airports...

Every corner of the earth, despite its natural beauty, is potentially affected by one or another of these actions. Any project which attempts to conscientiously, carefully deal with the question of environmental impact faces the same problem: how to reconcile its intended use while integrating it into its surroundings. There is no possible camouflage. This type of intervention involves civil engineering, and this means that the projects have to confront their influence on the site face on. The impact may be in an urban setting (the footbridge in Bilbao, or the acoustic wall in Miami) or of territorial scope (the A85 freeway in France or the Caminito de Rey in Malaga), but in both cases project development is based on similar mental mechanisms: the vistas created, topography which is modified with the utmost respect, and user relationships. An ever greater number of industrial terrains are also being rehabilitated on city outskirts, being turned into public park land with all the grassroots structural problems and specific environmental management this calls for: recycling, land pollution, urban design reclassification, program of uses, etc. Both groups are worthy of mention for the increasing awareness that certain operations cannot be carried out with total impunity, and have to be planned out to the finest detail, because they have far-reaching effects on all of our lives.

José A. Fernández-Ordoñez

Intervention in the Caminito del Rey

The Caminito del Rey passes through the two gorges of Gaitanejo and Los Gaitanes, areas that force us to reflect on the effects of man's intervention in nature. The conceptual question of how to intervene in an area of such extraordinary natural characteristics is the overriding problem of this project, and one that bears with it technical complexities that are difficult to resolve.

We all know that the explosion of technology has left its imprint on the natural world all over the planet. Even where man has not directly colonized an area, our intervention is palpable, as the area achieves a supposedly natural stability, and, due to the lack of normal human activity, becomes a place where the human will is manifest by its very absence. The gorges' interest lies in their geomorphology and not in the fact that they are untouched by the human hand. In fact, man's handiwork is more than evident: in some cases, like the railway which erupts into the space, it is only the immense natural force of the gorges which prevents their singular beauty from being cheapened. We had to ask ourselves questions about the relationship between this nature and our new path, about the form that a modern path, whose only function is to allow people to enjoy the area and appreciate its beauty, should take.

The engineering works from the past show great respect towards a still-untamed nature. The limit of these works was marked by an equilibrium between the ingenuity of the men who constructed them and the force of a nature difficult to dominate. The existing Caminito must have demanded great ingenuity and invention from builders who did not even have adequate materials —pieces of train rail had to be used as braces— or sufficient constructive resources. Undoubtedly the hesitant, rectilinear character of the path owes much to this lack of resources, and it is precisely this imposition of the rhythm of the construction on the very different character of the mountain, which causes conflict.

Our path follows the line laid down by our predecessors, but only traces of its impetus remain, as we have no need for a path from which to inspect the canal, or to shorten the distance between the dam and the workers' village in El Chorro, but only for one that allows us to enjoy the beauty of the zone.

In constructing this new path we wish to express a manner of approaching nature from a technical point of view and show how, in a natural space such as the gorges, technique must take a back seat and allow what is really important to show itself. The Caminito that we have designed is not just a simple path. We wanted it to become a way of looking and seeing. The path is supported by double brackets embedded in the rock face, which are built to the scale of the mountain rather than to a human one. The new path is separated from the limestone wall of the mountain and, supported by the brackets, runs almost parallel to it, imitating its movements. The brackets are made of steel, cast with an alloy of stainless steel and titanium, and bear up the structure of sheet steel which in turn supports the terrazzo paving. The structural box is curved for nearly all its length and molds itself smoothly to the irregularities of the mountainside without touching or seeking support from the rock.

The path measures a horizontal line along the rock face in an attempt to understand the mountain, acting as a kind of huge instrument which reproduces all the movements of the rock. It does not touch the wall of rock, but rather respects its force. If the path was embedded in the rock face it would belong only to one side of the gorge, but as built, it succeeds in distancing itself from both sides, seeing the gorge as a unified space, one to which it does not belong but merely passes through.

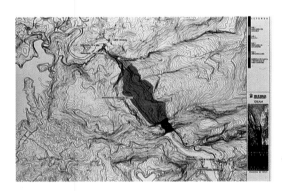

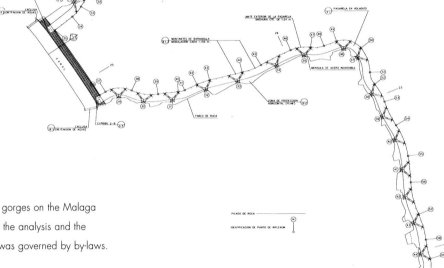

Situation of the gorges on the Malaga
Coast. Plans of the analysis and the
design, which was governed by by-laws.

Cross section of the original path.
The railings and the fixings have come
away from the rock.

Cross section of the new design for the Caminito.

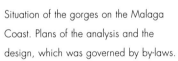

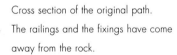

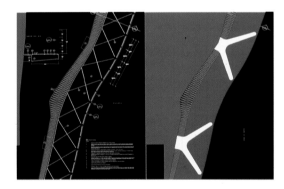

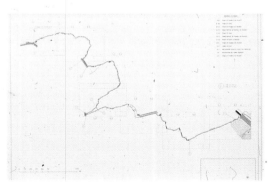

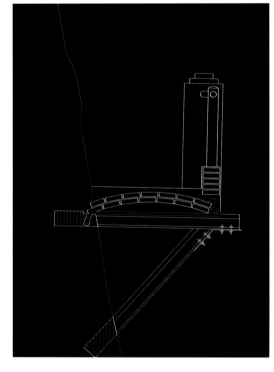

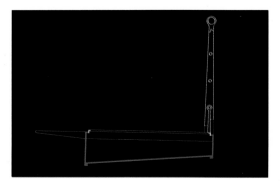

Brackets of stainless steel. Model.

Location: Desfiladero de los Gaitanes y del Gaitanejo,

Malaga, Spain.

Developer: Empresa Pública del Suelo de Andalucía,

Consejería de Obras Públicas y Transportes, Junta de Andalucía.

Head of Design of E.P.S.A: José Antonio Cobo Baro (architect).

Supervision: Miguel Moya, INASER S.L.

Head of team: José A. Fernández-Ordoñez

(civil engineer).

Design architects: L. Fernández-Ordoñez,

L.I. Bartolomé, D. Díaz, E. Khale.

Civil engineers: J. Martínez, F. Millanes, M. Delgado.

Date of design: 1996-1997.

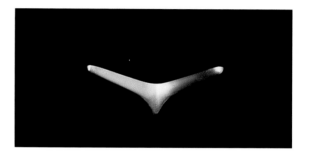

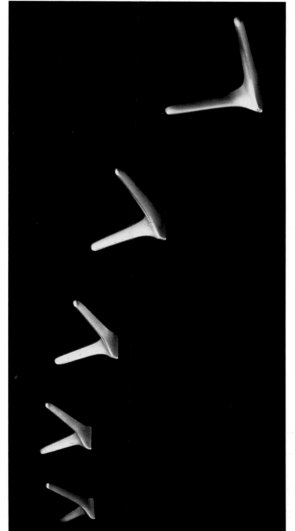

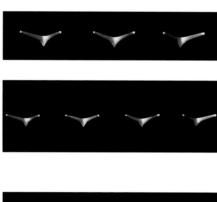

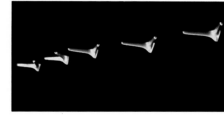

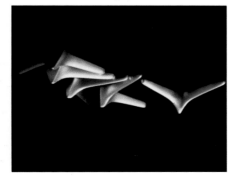

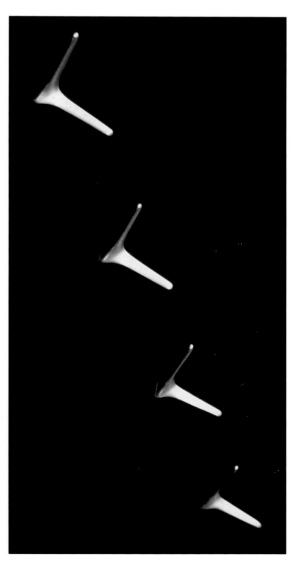

Santiago Calatrava Valls

Uribitarte Footbridge

Until recently the city of Bilbao was the major focus of industry in northern Spain and, in some sectors such as iron and steel, topped the national production tables. Since the seventies, however, Bilbao has been undergoing a major process of industrial conversion which has pushed it out of the competitive circuits of European cities. The industry, by now abandoned or with obsolete installations, occupies strategic development areas in the city.

The city is spread out along the river estuary. The great plants of the iron and steel, chemical and shipbuilding industries were set up on the banks of the river, forcing residential areas out to the hills and making for complex communications between the different areas of the city. The estuary, which is the backbone of the city, has always been a difficult obstacle to cross, separating the city into two socially differentiated areas.

The latest Partial Territorial Plan of Metropolitan Bilbao which is currently being introduced is based on the strategic construction of city-wide structural road elements on the old sites of large industries along the riverbank. The new development potential of the metropolis comprises flat sites, close to the water, with places to stimulate private investment and facilitate interconnection between the various parts of the city. Various projects have been designed to develop service areas, such as the plan for Abandoibarra by César Pelli & Ass., large new cultural amenities such as the Guggenheim Museum by F. Gehry & Ass. and the conference center by F. Soriano & Ass., or projects to improve the communications network such as the subway by N. Foster & Partners, an intermodal station by M. Wilford & Partners and the Uribitarte footbridge by Santiago Calatrava, who has also been commissioned to design the new airport terminal.

The Uribitarte footbridge spans the 73 meters from one side of the river to the other, continuing Calle Ercilla in the city extension to the other bank, where a large area of warehouses is being overhauled to adapt them, by the addition of two floors, for use as offices and apartments. The structure of the tensed arch is steel, just like the ribs which subject the totally glazed walkway. The metal structure is anchored to the ground by concrete elements which, with their characteristic shape, serve as ramps leading up to the level of the bridge. As the walkway does not lie exactly beneath the tensed arch, the support ribs balance out the torsion at the ends of the footbridge. The arch, reaching a height of 15 meters above water level, follows a different route to the walkway, supporting two focuses of cables, one to either side.

Calatrava's work as a builder of bridges stands head and shoulders above purely civil engineering to become architecture. His constant reformulation of the old questions raised by the need to span large distances leads him to solutions which follow the contemporary tradition of great bridge builders in the technical field, but the field of form takes him to the limits of a balance of forces, like a Gothic builder, without revealing whether it is form that follows function or vice versa. Moreover, his bridges do not meekly fit into cityscapes; they strike out for visible positions to become landmarks, radically changing the urban image and landscape of cities.

The balance of forces taken to the limit. An asymmetrical arch, a walkway with a double curve where the central nerve subjects ribs which extend as far as necessary in each position. The concrete abutments on the riverbanks double as ramps to reach the height of the walkway.

The 220-foot footbridge spans the estuary to join a residential area with warehouses and workshops, a sector in the process of conversion to mixed areas where workshops mingle with offices and houses.

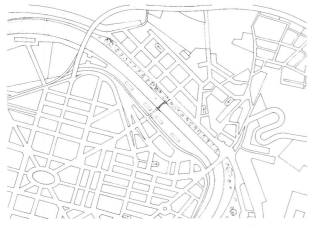

Ground plan of site on the Bilbao estuary.

Location: Uribitarte, Bilbao, Spain.

Client: City of Bilbao.

Span: 220 ft.

Date of project: 1990.

Date of construction: 1997.

Photograph: Jordi Miralles.

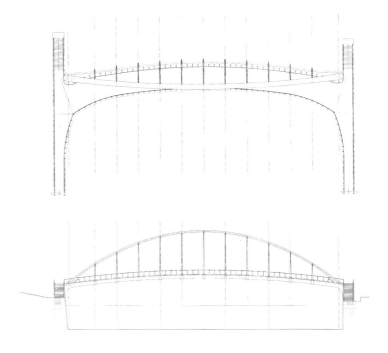

Preliminary design.

Bernard Lassus & Associates

Landscaping of the A85 Freeway

Bernard Lassus' design embraces all aspects relative to the impact of a new section of freeway on a countryside which is particularly attractive. The criteria of his design are based on the search for fresh and alternative solutions to the usual system of mechanically wrought cuttings and embankments which cleave through the countryside, severing the visual nexus between the driver and the surrounding landscape, and making the new highway appear as an unwelcome intrusion into the lives of the local inhabitants.

Lassus' design takes into account the visual point of view of both the driver and the local inhabitants, looking for ways in which both groups can experience a relationship with the resulting landscape. To this end he proposed two main areas of actuation in which to apply this strategy: the system of cuttings and embankments, and the construction of rest areas, specifically the service area that adjoins the Étang de Ténières, a new artificial lake created for the project. A third area of actuation, which complements the first, is the strategy used with respect to the vegetation and new plantations.

In his approach to the necessary cuttings and embankments, Lassus seeks an alternative to the well-used weapon of simply cleaving through the existing topography to make way for the new road. As an alternative, he offers a meticulous study which envisages the new topographical order in three dimensions, so that the transition between the new planes generated by the construction and the surrounding landscape should have as much continuity as possible. At the points where the freeway follows a gradient very different from that of the surrounding topography, Lassus proposes a series of interrupted cuttings that allow the driver to see the surrounding countryside at certain points. At other points, such as the Corzé interchange, the architect uses a new three-dimensional strategy of slopes and embankments so that the landscape, the elongated strand of freeway and the system of planes which unite them are brought together with a maximum of continuity.

The strategy of modifying the existing topography is accompanied by a parallel strategy that accompanies and completes it: the treatment of the vegetation and the new plantations of trees. At some points, Lassus has established copses of trees, but ones which run perpendicular to the road, again permitting glimpses of the far horizon and ensuring that this new element does not act as another factor which cuts off the view. At other points, such as the long straight stretches of freeway, Lassus proposes the planting of trees parallel to the road but set right back, so that the vegetation seems to define some great channel with the freeway proper at its center. The space between the trees and the road is occupied by fields, and where these slope, they do so smoothly and gently. In the end, the fields and the vegetation become the principal components of Lassus' design and the dry, featureless, truncated embankments so often seen on freeways disappear. Once again, the effect of the disappearance of this screen means that the vegetation, the fields, the vision of the driver and the experiences of the local inhabitants are integrated in one continuum.

Pursuing the same ideal of connecting the freeway with the land, the architect uses an artificial lake around which to build a rest area, a bridge between the experience of driving and that of being in the country. The Étang des Ténières rest area has the lake as its center, where it is possible to use the small boats provided or even to swim from the small artificial beaches. So, the main leisure element of the area is the water itself, a natural element which integrates easily into the landscape.

The main interest of Lassus' design is that it can be typified and extrapolated to other circumstances, as it addresses a problem –the integration of major highways into the landscape– which is omnipresent in our modern-day society and which has in the past been the cause of major contradictions, which this design seeks to resolve or at least tone down.

Conceptual photomontages.
The existing trees are pointed up
by the planting of new additions
to create an impression of woodland.

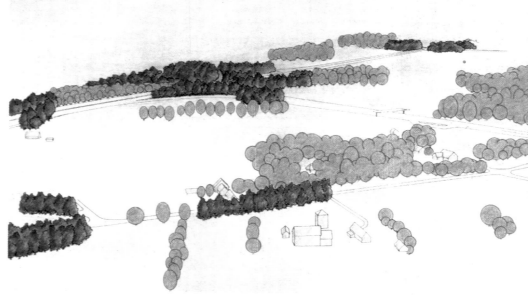

In some cases, the new plantations of trees are placed perpendicular to the road, which provides drivers with a vision of the horizon and thus an overall perception of the country through which they pass.

Location: A85 freeway,
Angers-Tours-Vierzon, France.
Client: Société Cofiroute.
Length: 138 miles.
Date of design: 1996.
Date of construction: 1997.

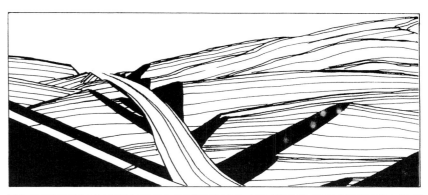

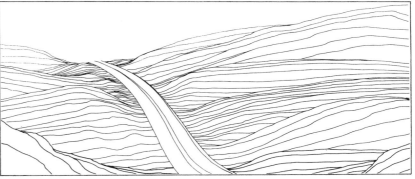

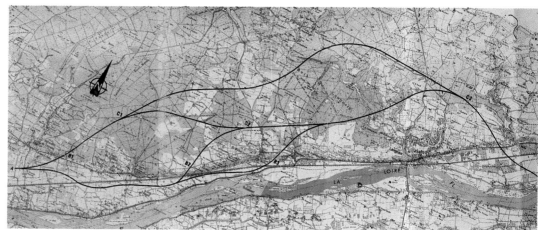

Project plans for a detailed
study of the topography and the
embankments created.

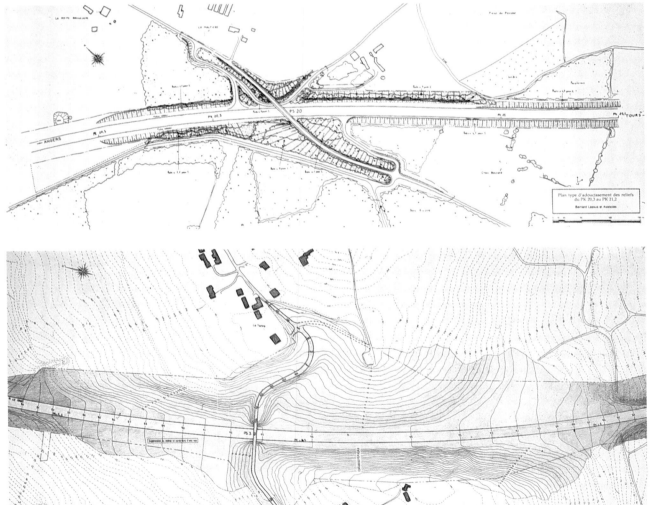

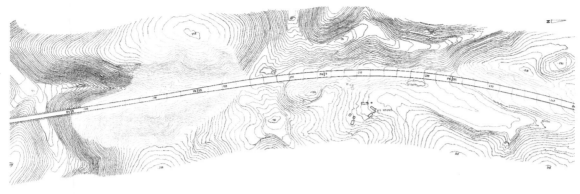

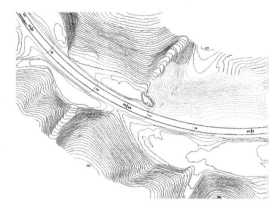

LEGENDE — Courbes de niveau du T.N. équidistance de 2.00 m.   Courbes de niveau en déblais par rapport au T.N. équidistance de 2.00 m.   Courbes de niveau en remblais par rapport au T.N. équidistance de 2.00 m.

LEGENDE — Courbes de niveau du T.N. équidistance de 2.00 m.   Courbes de ni équidistance d

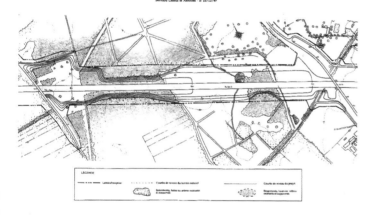

Autoroute A.85 Tours - Vierzon
Extrait du plan du grand déblai de Langeais au PK 100.5
Hypothèse dans laquelle les terrassements restent dans l'emprise
Bernard Lassus et Associés - le 15/12/97

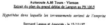

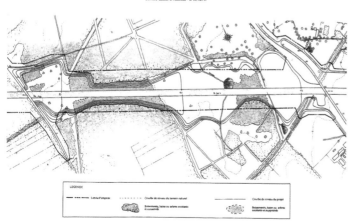

Autoroute A.85 Tours - Vierzon
Extrait du plan du grand déblai de Langeais au PK 100.5
Hypothèse dans laquelle les terrassements sortent de l'emprise
Bernard Lassus et Associés - le 15/12/97

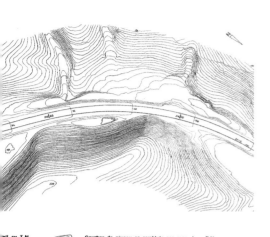

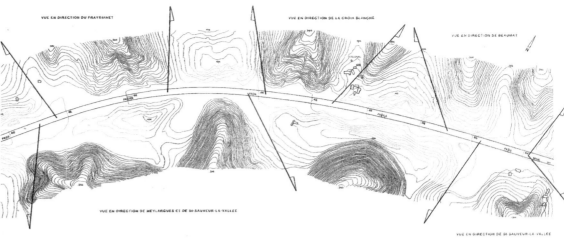

VUE EN DIRECTION DU FRAYSSINET VUE EN DIRECTION DE LA CROIX BLANCHE VUE EN DIRECTION DE BEAUMAT

VUE EN DIRECTION DE MEYLARGUES ET DE St-SAUVEUR-LA-VALLÉE

VUE EN DIRECTION DE St-SAUVEUR-LA-VALLÉE

LÉGENDE

Courbes de niveau du T.N.
équidistance de 2.00 m.

Courbes de niveau en déblais par rapport au T.N.
équidistance de 2.00 m.

Courbes de niveau en remblais par rapport au T.N.
équidistance de 2.00 m.

art au T.N.

Courbes de niveau en remblais par rapport au T.N.
équidistance de 2.00 m.

0 50 m.   200 m.   500 m.

In the Corzé interchange, the rearranging of the topography has been carried out using three-dimensional criteria, adapting the new relief to the route of the road and so avoiding the necessity of screen-like embankments which disrupt the view.

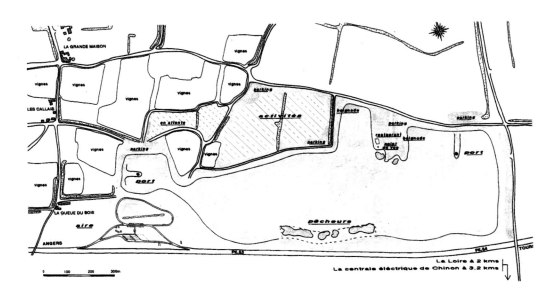

De

. l'Etang des Ténières à la découverte du pays.

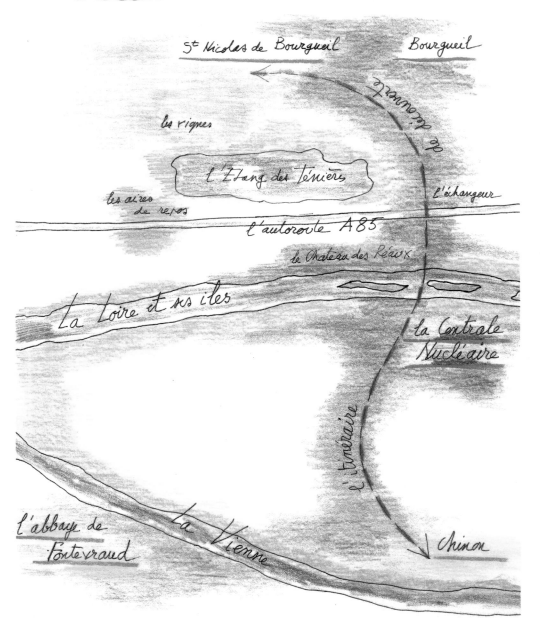

Bernard Larrue Juillet 96

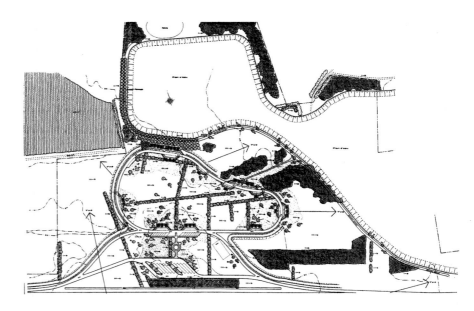

General layout for the Étang des
Ténières area and detail of the north-
and southbound rest areas on the A85
freeway between Angers and Tours.

Martha Schwartz, Inc.

Acoustic Wall

Colored glass and sunlight bring to life this wall, designed for noise suppression which runs for roughly a mile along 36th Street, at the northern limit of Miami International Airport. The wall, which separates the airport from two adjoining neighborhoods, was considered essential by the airport management but was at first vehemently rejected by the neighbors. The idea of having a long wall whose height varies between 18 and 30 feet ring one's neighborhood is a radical, artificial and contentious one that is, understandably, difficult to accept, even if it results in a considerable reduction in noise pollution. The challenge to the designer was to transform the inevitability of the wall's construction into something at least minimally acceptable to the occupants of the zones affected.

An added problem was that the side of the wall which would be visible to the neighbors was north-facing, which meant that any type of painting, mural, bas-relief or graffiti would have resulted in a decorated wall in permanent shadow. Martha Schwartz's design takes advantage of this unfavorable orientation by using sunlight as the main dynamizing element of the construction. Small windows of colored glass are placed between the pillars of the reinforced concrete, which allow the sunlight to pass through, tinting it with a variety of colors.

To avoid monotony in the distribution of spaces and colors, six different designs of pre-fabricated panels were used, which allowed many possible combinations. Likewise, the upper undulation of the wall was varied to attenuate as far as possible the brutal force conveyed by a wall of these dimensions. The dimensions of the wall are varied both by the undulations at the top and at the bottom where the construction is adapted to meet the varying slopes and gradients of the ground. The apparent disorder that characterizes the wall for most of its length is transformed by a reorganization of the colored windows into a screen that surrounds the main entrance to the airport. Both this change in distribution of the windows in the final section and the changes in the panels along the wall's length help to imbue the construction with a sense of movement in an attempt to avoid the monotony which might seem inevitable in an operation of this kind.

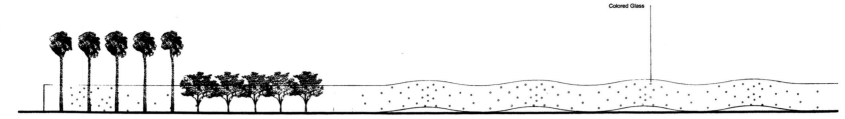

Colored Glass

Elevation.

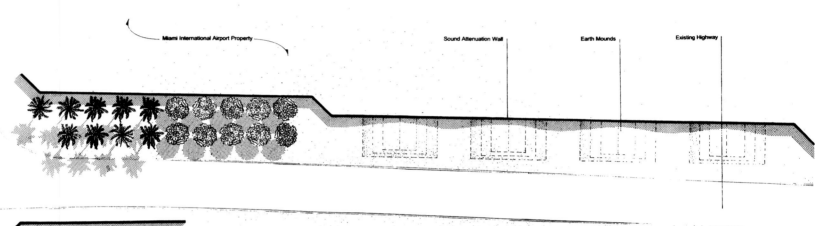

Miami International Airport Property

Sound Attenuation Wall

Earth Mounds

Existing Highway

Ground plan.

0   100 FEET

N

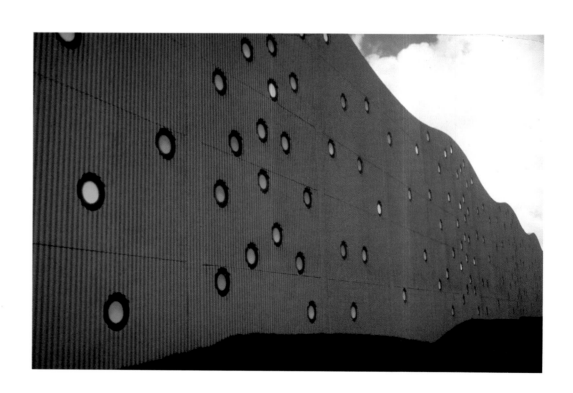

Location: Miami, Florida, USA.

Client: Metro-Dade Art in Public Places.

Date: 1996.

Photographs: Kevin Conger, Paula Meijerink,
Martha Schwartz.

Hargreaves Associates

Parque do Tejo e Trançao

This project was the winning design in an ideas competition for a park beside the planned site for Expo '98 in Lisbon. The park is situated on the banks of the river Tajo which were formerly used for industry, waste processing and refuse dumps. It is becoming more and more common to find industrial wasteland being put to other uses as saturated urban zones seek room to expand. The basic problem in these cases is always where to find the necessary funding for costly and protracted processes. The prospect of an international event will obviously provide the impetus needed, and in this case the advent of the 1998 World Fair has smoothed the way for this project.

The idea here was to turn this rundown, abandoned site into a park which, without attempting to erase the place's history, was capable of appreciating the significance of industrial areas and introducing an environmental education program with the direct involvement of local residents who visit the park. Additionally, Hargreaves Associates outlined an extensive brief of recreational uses: a piazza for festivals and popular events, playing fields, a golf course, horse riding amenities, tennis and volleyball courts, a fun fair, shops and cafes.

The principal formal argument of the design lies in the sculptural manipulation of the land into dunes and earthworks of different shapes which are laid out according to their location in the park, seeking to give a functional and symbolic explanation.

In terms of function, the project had to find space for some 18 million cubic feet of sediment from the port; symbolically the silt adopts forms which could have been sculpted by the area's enduring wind. These undulations, metaphorical waves, are also reminiscent of the meeting of sea and earth, graduating from artificial to natural; the berms along the river look almost natural, as though sculpted by wind and water, yet the further we penetrate into the park, the more artificial they become, quite unambiguously expressing their manmade origins. This graduation also serves as a framework of reference for the various uses which are located in one place or another according to their characteristics.

The project also includes an existing sewage treatment plant, and has special measures for dealing with the odors produced so as not to affect use of the park. Another element in the brief was the tertiary treatment of water to allow the marshlands and their natural habitat of flora and fauna to recover their historical and ecological significance. The topographical make-up of these areas allows visitors to come into direct contact with the animals and plants that live at the meeting of earth and water.

The project for the Parque do Tejo e Trançao is not an attempt to "cure" a "wounded" area and return it to its natural state; this would be little more than a simulation of a past which ceased to exist a long time ago. The park is actually a place which has been recycled for public use, a place where ecological, urban development and economic interests all come together.

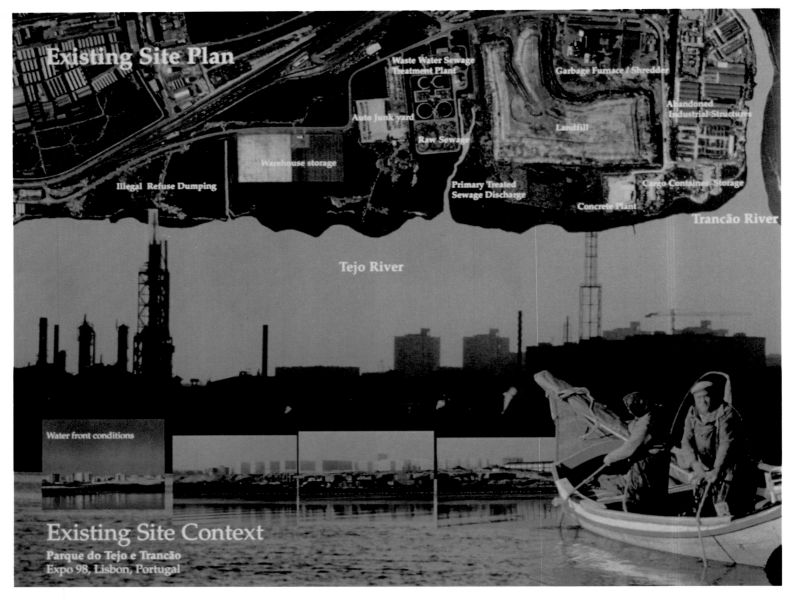

Existing Site Plan

Waste Water Sewage
Treatment Plant

Garbage Furnace / Shredder

Auto Junk yard

Landfill

Abandoned
Industrial Structures

Warehouse storage

Raw Sewage

Illegal Refuse Dumping

Primary Treated
Sewage Discharge

Cargo Container Storage

Concrete Plant

Trancão River

Tejo River

Water front conditions

Existing Site Context

Parque do Tejo e Trancão
Expo 98, Lisbon, Portugal

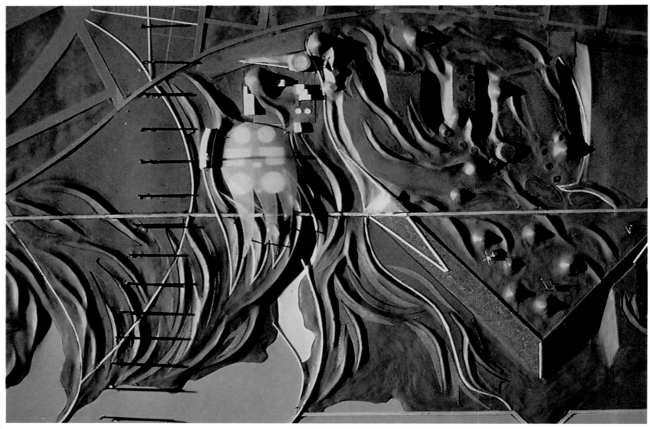

O Aterro

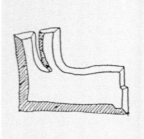 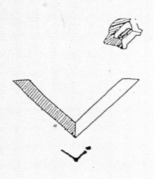  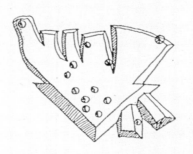

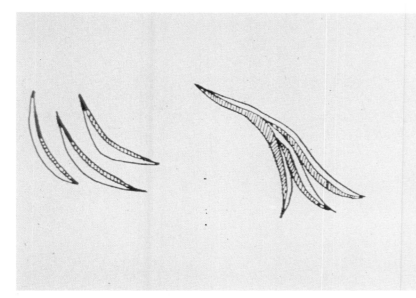 

The cone-shaped, wind-formed elements play a dual role in the project: function (they are the end product of dredging the port) and symbol (as a representation of the persistent presence of the wind in the area).

Previous page:
One of the panels presented in the international competition for the park, won by Hargreaves Associates.

Location: Lisbon, Portugal.

Surface: 160 acres.

Project date: 1994-1998.

Completion date: Spring 1998.

Photograph: Hargreaves Associates.

Latz & Partner

Duisburg-Nord Park

This project for Duisburg-Nord Park forms part of a huge green zone in the region of Emscher, currently being developed for the International Architecture Exhibition which is to be held in 1999 (IBA). Together with the cities in the region of Emscher, the German Federal State of Nordrhein-Westfalen have brought several projects into operation with a view to refurbishing old industrial areas in the Ruhr basin.

The Duisburg-Nord park is situated between the cities of Meiderich and Hamborn in an area of heavy industries (coal and steel) between the urban agglomerations of Duisburg and Oberhausen in the Ruhr basin, one of the country's major industrial areas with a population of 5 million inhabitants. The former site of the Thyssen foundry has preserved all the paraphernalia of an industry of these characteristics: smelting furnace, warehouses, and rail installations, now in disuse.

An international competition announced in 1990 was won by Latz & Partner with the aim of totally updating the area to provide its dense population with recreational, sports and cultural amenities set in a landscape which recovers the old industrial installations; this project appreciates the complex's enormous value in terms of history but also as an act of archaeological research into industry. The remains of the old industrial installations are preserved as a valuable heritage, at the same time being made available for public enjoyment; they are now symbols of the park and necessary landmarks in their vast area of influence. One of the initial ideas was to turn these huge remains into integral elements of the park, places to be used and enjoyed by the inhabitants.

These fragmented, rundown structures were never meant to be reconstructed. They present certain independent systems with potentially functional connections in some cases, in others visual or merely ideal. A railway park with raised walkways, an aquatic park at its lowest point, promenades crossing the park to link the various city districts and elements to connect main sectors such as small gardens, terraces, towers, footbridges and plazas.

The magnitude of the project called for a piece-by-piece interventions which are opened to the public as they are completed. As far as possible, on-site materials have been used, both directly and recycled, as in the case of the iron in the footbridges, platforms and gates. Other materials have been used for paving or concrete mixtures for new walls, and the huge hematite sheets which cover the ground of the Piazza Metallica are taken from the smelting furnaces. The elements which have been developed to date are the footbridges to connect different parts of the park, certain stretches of the system of water courses, gardens and patios occupied by the old mineral deposits, and singular spots such as Cowper Place, Piazza Metallica, the theater and Stonehall Place which occupy characteristic sites in the factory's construction system. Separate gardens have also been laid out with a variety of plant life and even, with the participation of local inhabitants, small box-gardens which reuse waste materials from the production process to study possible types of vegetation which could be planted in the park.

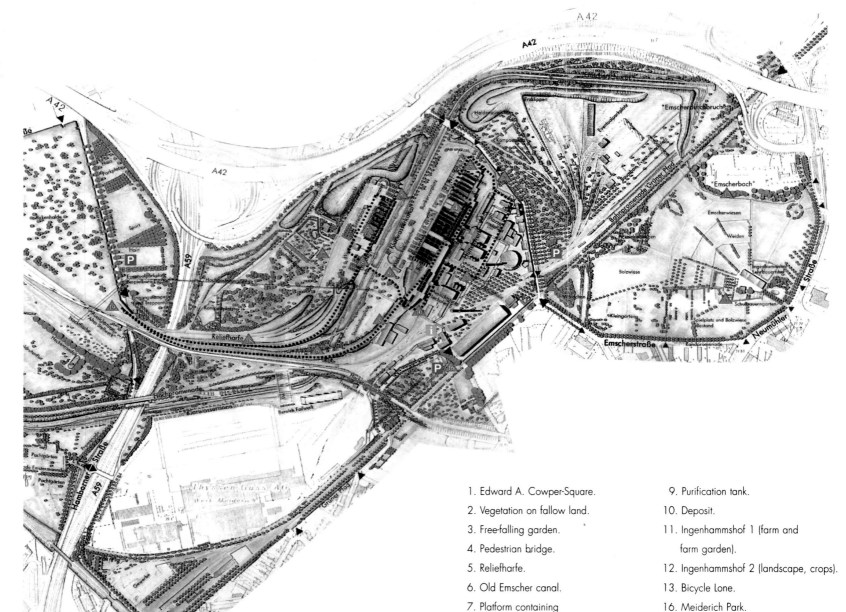

1. Edward A. Cowper-Square.
2. Vegetation on fallow land.
3. Free-falling garden.
4. Pedestrian bridge.
5. Reliefharfe.
6. Old Emscher canal.
7. Platform containing metal deposits.
8. Sythesization plants.
9. Purification tank.
10. Deposit.
11. Ingenhammshof 1 (farm and farm garden).
12. Ingenhammshof 2 (landscape, crops).
13. Bicycle Lone.
16. Meiderich Park.
17. Hamborn Park.
▲ Entrances.

Location: Duisburg, Nordrhein-Westfalen, Germany.

Client: Development Company of Nordrhein-Westfalen and tha city of Duisburg.

Surface area: 230 hectares.

Collaborating groups: IBA (Internationale Bauaustellung), IG Nordpark, Society for Industrial Culture and the Parks Department of Duisburg City Council.

Date of project: 1990 (competition).

Date of construction: 1991-2000.

Photographs: Latz & Partner, Christa Panick, Peter Wilde, Michael Latz y Angus Parker.

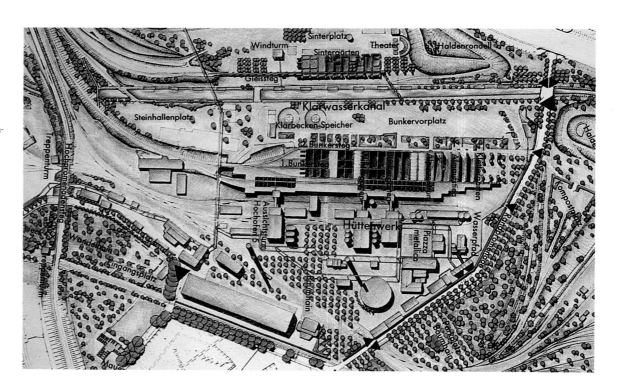

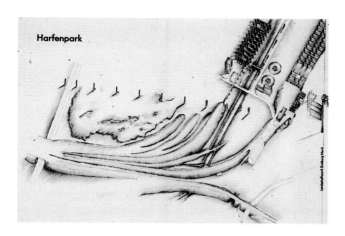

Harfenpark

The old railway lines have been
transformed into green paths.
Only their form recalls their old use.

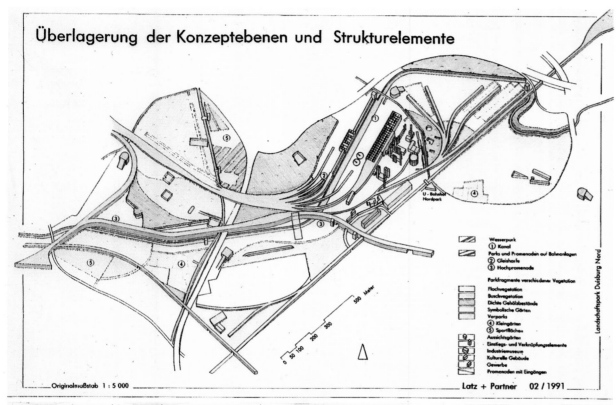

Überlagerung der Konzeptebenen und Strukturelemente

Originalmaßstab 1 : 5 000

Latz + Partner   02 / 1991

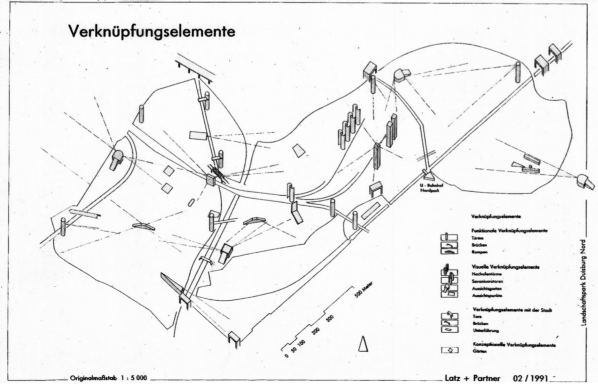

Verknüpfungselemente

Originalmaßstab 1 : 5 000

Latz + Partner   02 / 1991

Diagrams of the different systems
of communications and zoning
and their relationship with the
existing landmark buildings.

Cowper Place.

On the following page:
Piazza Metallica. This singular spot
reveals the potential for metamorphosis
of factory installations. A quiet square
surrounded by yards of piping, tanks
and chimneys, with space for
vegetation. The paving in the center
finds a good use for huge sheets of
hematite, each weighing over 7 tons,
originally part of the smelting furnaces.

The old mineral deposit areas have been turned into small patios and gardens.

Free-falling garden.

The aquatic park. A canal, which uses the bed of an old main drain, crosses the park from east to west. A network of clean water is provided for the various gardens, using wind-powered energy.

Breiter Klarwasserkanal

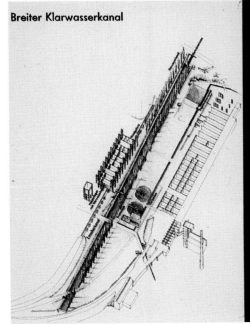

A pile of waste materials, grassed over and planted, now provides a vantage point over the park.

One of the walkways and theater which take advantage of the shape of on old crater.

An old synthesis plant was demolished because of contamination. In its place, beside the remains of an old chimney, new gardens and a plantation of *Ailanthus Altissima* flourishes on the recycled plot.

The mineral deposit gardens are built at different levels. The walls of the deposits –two meters thick– had to be perforated to provide access and communicate them.

An area of the port which reuses the railway installations. Moss and lichens grow amongst the rubbish.

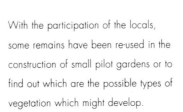

With the participation of the locals, some remains have been re-used in the construction of small pilot gardens or to find out which are the possible types of vegetation which might develop.

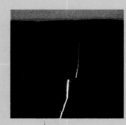

LAND ART

The first works carried out by the exponents of Land Art, in the late 60s and early 70s, had a slow but sure influence which gradually reached to the very heart of architecture: so much so that nearly all architectural projects nowadays have a landscape component. An intermediate step in this process has been the institutionalization of so-called "landscape architecture" which is now taught in universities and colleges, with its corresponding degrees and diplomas, and whose concrete application can be seen in the extremely practical designs that now accompany any architectural transformation or intervention.

If landscape architecture is now applied as a discipline in fields which encroach on architecture itself, genuine Land Art, in its purest conception as an intervention or alteration of a place without any aim except that of perturbing our vision (and hence our experience), has pursued another path. In some cases, it takes the form of a celebration of nature, with the artist aesthetically translating its formal potential; in other cases, it seeks a provocative disruption which challenges the conformity of the viewer; some artists look for ways to immerse the human form in the most inaccessible places, while others use their art as a critique of the traditional urban landscape, using elements which disrupt its presumed harmony.

The works which are presented here can all be fitted into one of these categories, although they all have in common the desire to influence people's consciousness through their vision, the sense that most connects us with our surroundings.

The "0 m. Panel", defined as "the first element of a transection, a system of references which allows botanists and geologists to determine the beginning of something so as to be able to make measurements decade after decade from this starting point", may be placed in any location as the starting point for a new intervention.

Paul-Armand Gette

Rubia Peregrina L. - 0 m. Panel - Parc de Gourjade

Paul-Armand Gette is an artist whose self-taught knowledge of the natural sciences —mineralogy, botany and the aspects of bio-climatology related to the natural landscape— has led him to contemplate his work from a perspective that is scientific rather than concerned with visual perception. This interest, developed in museums of science and through a questioning approach towards all the elements that compose the reality of nature —especially rocks and vegetation— has, little by little, become focused on the specifically dimensional aspects of the elements. The result is that Gette has reached the point where he develops his work as if it were a study of the elements carried out by processes of measurement, always linked to the parallel processes of growth, assumption of form and optimum biological development. This has led him to clearly understate the purely visual aspects, purifying them until they become a completely anti-formal contemplation of the elements of which nature is composed, a contemplation which has more to do with an appreciation of their reality it itself than seeing them as products of an artistic or aesthetic intervention. Commenting on these processes of perception on the subject of his project **Rubia Peregrina L.**, Gette writes: "If designing means leaving a mark, then this gesture in itself is enough, and so is extending a pointing finger, writing a small text on a ticket, or both. I often ask my models to show, in an engaging way, what they most wish to call attention to, although I also hope that the vision of the spectator loses itself in the model, that for a brief instant they are distracted, that perhaps they want to touch, as I like doing myself."

This overriding interest in dimensional variables led Gette to establish the so-called **"0 m. Panel"** which he himself defines as "the first element of a transection, a system of references which allows botanists and geologists to determine the beginning of something to be able to make measurements decade after decade from this starting point". This panel, which is incorporated in different ways in all his works, marks, in a strictly conceptual way, the dimensional point of the beginning of an intervention, a "Greenwich Mean" for the new system of co-ordinates which serve as the base for the actuation. In this way Gette re-emphasizes the importance of the measurable variable as the guideline which conditions his work, free from formal display or the concept of a landscape conceived along aesthetic lines.

In his design for the **Parc de Gourjade**, Gette used a complex method based on the manipulation of various measurements to determine the planting of 31 new trees which he defines as the "high arborescent strata of the place". The importance of the new plantation is the elevated arboreal mass which it will generate, a new volume which has to maintain a physical relation with the place and with all the existing geological and topographical elements. Gette's starting point was a meticulous dimensional study of the rocks of the river Agout which runs by the park, mainly with regard to their length, width and density. This led him to fix a series of 31 boulders which are exhibited didactically in a panel, a series whose number and siting determine for him the number and position of the new trees. In addition, a system of analogical relationships between the characteristics of the boulders will determine the different species to be planted.

In this way, Gette operates digitally, in a logical, abstract system of relationships in which all the elements of the natural world cohere globally and organically. Previously, Gette has carried out various projects with large rocks, studying their morphology and placing them as monoliths in keeping with an intimate understanding of their natural form. For Gette, a thorough understanding of the elements which make up nature comes from a strictly limited intuition of their organic harmony, their vitality, their measurable variables and their morphology. The design for the Parc de Gourjade is presented as a "phyto-ornamental proposal". This expression indicates the leading role that the science of phytography plays in the design, together with its aesthetic character, and the addition of the conceptual aspect of intuition which underlies the whole project.

Rubia Peregrina L.
Labeling in the Bois de Crestet.
Art Center, 1994.
Marking, labeling, identifiying and
pointing out are Gette's means of
acting on reality and conscionsly
perceiving it differently.

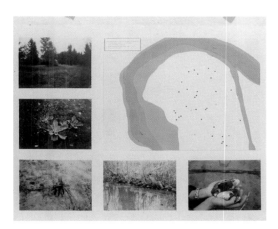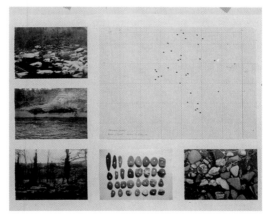

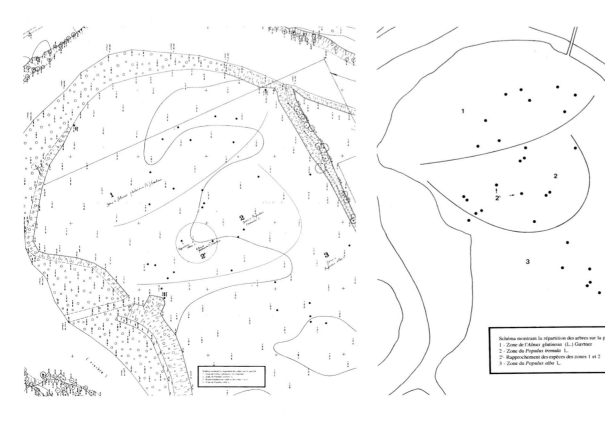

Gette uses the procedure of showing systems of classification, partitions etc., as in the scientific method, to illustrate his way of working in the **Parc de Goujarde**. The lower left panel shows the 31 boulders which serve as the classificatory basis for planting the new trees.

Location: Castres, France.

Client: Castres City Council.

Date of project: 1996.

Date of completion: 1997.

Photographs: Monika Nikolic, Paul-Patrik Gette, Paul-Armand Gette.

Diagram showing the distribution of trees over the terrain.

1. Zone of *Alnus glutinosa*.

2. Zone of *Populus tremula*.

2'. Species of zones 1 and 2.

3. Zona de *Populus alba*.

Monika Gora

A volume of light - Jimmys

These two installations by Monika Gora illustrate the main characteristics of her work in their implicit interpretation of the city and the conception of a potentially ephemeral intervention in it using a landscape architecture approach. The first, **A volume of light**, is a great elongated, aerodynamic globe of light, measuring 90x30x25 feet with three sulfur lamps inside it, posted in the middle of a major traffic junction in Vienna; the varying influences of the piece's great luminosity on its surroundings (in addition to the various phases of the sun on the globe at different times of day) are, in themselves, enough to create a focus of attention. The second installation, **Jimmys**, is intended for use for children's games in a public place, although its size and formal ambiguity make it appropriate for adults, too. It consists of a collection of pieces of different heights (between 1 1/2 and 4 1/2 feet) in orange, yellow and green plastic which relate eccentrically to the human body. As they are arranged on a flat surface in groups of up to ten pieces, they also create an impact on the surrounding cityscape.

Both of these interventions share a desire to intervene on given spots of the historical city in an unusual, unexpected and downright provocative fashion and to provoke reactions of disconcertion, surprise, pleasure and perhaps even contradiction in the random spectator-users. Monika Gora creates a counterpoint to the austere materials of the old urban landscape by introducing materials from industrial sources which are quite foreign to traditional construction. Her aim is to make its appearance undergo a metamorphosis with the passing hours, depending on the various nuances of sunlight, and the change from day to night-time. Monika Gora's announcement-objects tend to generate their own luminosity at night, becoming autonomous spotlights that illuminate everything around them. The great globe in Vienna shines with its own light at night-time, like the elements that make up Jimmys, which have small lamps hung inside them that shine through the thin plastic sheet to produce light-filled objects.

The work of Monika Gora consists of working out a fantasy which eludes the "whys and wherefores" of the things we do and calls out to our capacity to marvel or be surprised. This is the raison d'être of the installations with which she intervenes in the traditional city, establishing a convulsive relationship with the spectator-passerby. Her objects oppose the necessary search for "whys and wherefores" which run through the entire rationalist construction tradition; they are the product of a pure imagination which denies and even challenges this tradition. This explains her liking for mutable appearances, the observation of changing qualities of light during the course of the day, the nuancing —in some cases actual confusion— of natural and artificial light, or for ephemeral objects designed to exist for just a few days. These processes of intervention are intended to give our everyday physical surroundings precisely what they are lacking: mobility, on-going transformation, variable luminosity, unsuspected relations with the human body.

And this is also why Monika Gora likes to work with completely unwonted materials in traditional construction: she uses synthesizing materials, plastics and even intangible materials like ice to build landmarks in which the fantastic presence of certain objects can only be related to the exceptional nature of a moment or the experience of extraordinary effects, never to what is constructed, thought or reasoned. In Monika Gora's art, the world of all that is solid, permanent, and the world of extraordinary experiences in which she locates her work, are clearly separated; if they are not in open opposition, at least the former acts as a basis for everyday life and the latter as an activating device for unusual experiences.

The objects in **Jimmys** are both a provocative intervention on the landscape and an attempt to throw a different light on children's games, as well as extending this concept to a new relationship with adults' bodies.

Location: Pildammsparken-Zenithgatan 12-14, Malmö, Sweden.

Date: 1996.

Photographs: Veronika Borg, Monika Gora, Jimmy Söderling.

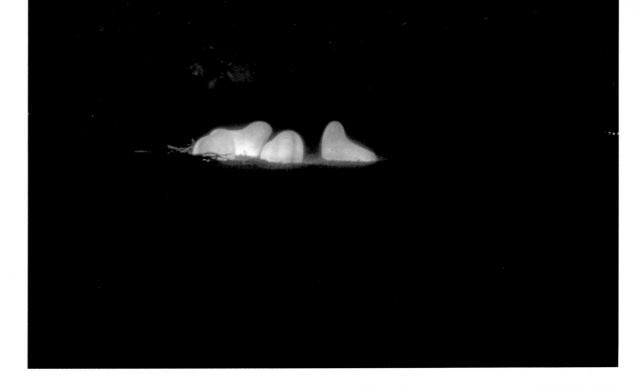

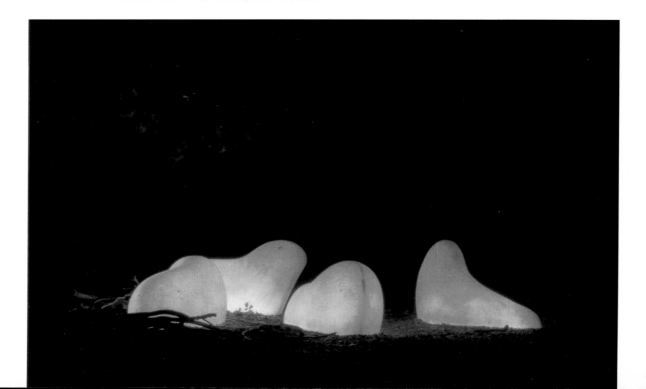

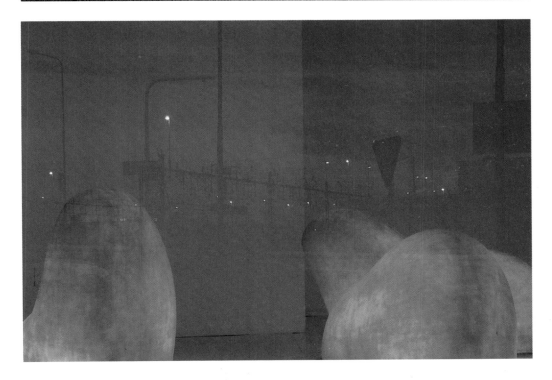

The great light-filled globe of **A volume of light** in Vienna's Schottentor touches all its surroundings with its light at night-time, while during the day its white surface provides a screen for the changing mutations of sunlight.

Location: Schottentor, Vienna, Austria.

Sponsor: Fusion Lighting, Inc.

Collaborator: Lars Bylund.

Date: 1995.

Photographs: Maria Hellström, Jimmy Söderling.

Hiroshi Nakao

Gisant/Transi

This object by Hiroshi Nakao takes its place in the Japanese tradition of setting architectural pieces in natural surroundings, mechanisms for the immersion of body and mind with a view to meditative or introspective states. In this case, the theme selected for the object was sleep and repose. Nakao defines his piece as a shelter for two beds "in a night of half sleep".

The basic matrix for the conception of the object is planimetric, so its final capsular appearance is the result of vertically raising this planimetric scheme. What is more, the ground plan defines the motions of movements and rotation which are to determine the use of the object; ultimately the plan is more like a sketch or an ideogram than a truly spatial conception.

If we initially consider this planimetric conception apart from the place where the object is to be sited, it draws out a series of coordinates which divide the space it theoretically occupies into four quadrants. Each of these four quadrants is occupied by a different object, although depending on how we see them, they can be grouped into twos. The smaller two objects are directed outwards so that their inner faces are more closed and the outer ones more open, in the form of bars which suggest a cage. The bars are far enough apart, however, to nuance this idea, allowing Nakao to introduce one of the favorite mechanisms of his installation: a play on ambiguities and indeterminacy. The other two slightly larger objects are more or less U-shaped and directed inwards. Here it is the outer faces which hint at enclosure, while the inner ones open up by repeating the bar procedure. The idea expressed here is that of a cell, but so ambiguously that at no point is it explicitly declared.

This basic design, expressed in the planimetric scheme, sees each one of the four objects arranged in a quadrant, and proposes a simultaneous movement of all four from completely closed to absolutely open to create an empty space with a square ground plan on the inside.

The sleeping platforms allow the occupant to lie down inside the mechanism, to relate to the place and embark on his own process of meditation. As the detonator of this act of meditation, Nakao's object seeks to contain all the nuances, richness and subtlety of the thought it sets out to stimulate. Whether beside or inside the object, the occupant should find its spatiality sufficiently complex and indeterminate for his "half sleep", meditation or introspection to flow harmoniously.

Hiroshi Nakao's object is raised into the air to produce an extremely ambiguous object, basically capsular in structure and set in a fairly flat clearing in a wood. This serves to emphasize the architectural characteristics of the object, as in spite of its complexity, it is comprised of very few components: surfaces and openings marked out by bars. These few ingredients, subject to intense elaboration, along with the many possibilities suggested by their movement, come together to create a place charged with suggestion and nuance: somehow, the conventional elements of architecture are used to satisfy needs which, in this case, are of a strictly spiritual nature.

Nevertheless, the mechanism designed by Hiroshi Nakao will always be reducible to the information in the plans which define it: shadows, random, mysterious profiles which move over the surface (of the paper or the wood) in obedience to a fundamentally geometric law. It is this idea of the "shadow" and the "play of shadows" on a surface that underlies the author's technique in designing the object.

The basic purpose of the mechanism is the sleep of its occupant, a "half sleep" of meditation and introspection. The only programmatic element of the object is the two beds inside a capsular structure which sets out to suggest both cell and cage.

Location: Karuizawa,
Nagano, Japan.
Date: 1997.
Photographs: Nacasa & Partners inc.

Using just a few architectural elements
(planes and rows of bars), Nakao
manages to create an object of great
spatial complexity, thanks to his use
of ambiguity and nuance and the
multiplicity of possible positions.

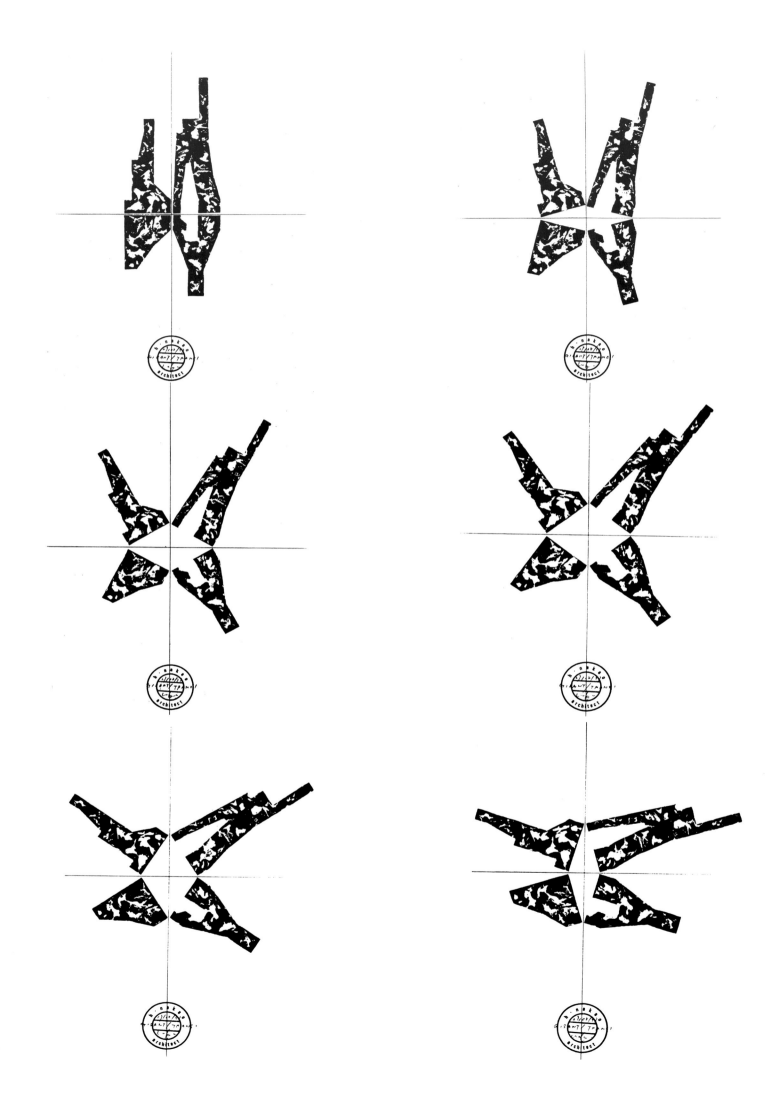

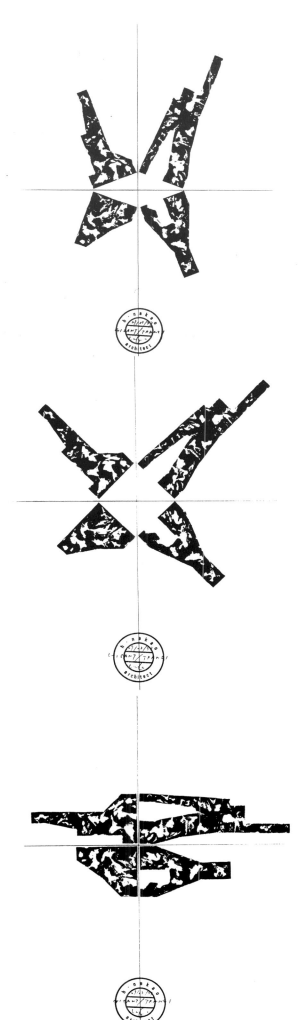

The Cartesian plan underlying the
design of the installation defines two
objects, each with a small mouth and
subdivisible into two, and framed by
axes of coordinates which will
determine their laws of motion.

Magdalena Jetelová

Iceland Project - Atlantik Wall - Dislocation

Three recent works by the Czech artist Magdalena Jeletová are presented here. The three are located in very different environments: a mountain range, a beach and a city.

Iceland Project. After a detailed study of Iceland's geology, a concept was developed to visualize the intercontinental divide which separates Eurasia and America. Iceland is the only place in the world where it is possible to see the Atlantic Mountain Chain which divides the two continental plates, running for more than 10,000 miles under the ocean and only emerging to cross the island for more than 220 miles.

In the summer of 1992, Magdalena Jeletová, together with a small group of experts, travelled to Iceland to identify and represent this geographical frontier between America and Eurasia. The dividing line was re-drawn from one end of the island to the other, using a laser beam. The photographs of this exercise form a documentary record of this laser frontier traced on the rocky ground, climbing and falling among the magmatic ranges and dissolving and disappearing among the steam of the geysers.

The minimal line the laser traces over the ground is representative of both our intellectual and conceptual systemization of our environment and the random character of natural formations. However, the artist considers this actuation not as an end in itself, but as part of a global process. The division, the fracturing into two parts, offers a hope of renewal. The surprising division of Iceland into two parts gives it a renewed beauty. The luminous dividing line traced upon the earth becomes part of it; without its presence, the earth cannot exist in this form, and it is this total interdependence that makes the work so fascinating.

Atlantik-Wall. The place is a beach on the North Sea coast of Denmark; its history marks it as a site of old battles which have left the remains of bunkers from World War II. Among the ruins which have survived the force of the waves, laser projections form phrases which speak to us of the meetings and partings which have taken place there. The aim is to present what already exists without any more manipulation than the impressions that the words may leave. However, the word by itself is not enough: it needs a stage. The interaction between the two produces the work. As in the previous work, the camera documents processes that are more global in nature. Once the work is documented, it can be developed in another time and place. The clash of opposites, the word against barbarism, acting in diverging planes, producing yet another new work in the place where they coincide.

Dislocations. This work formed part of a group exhibition organized in the Museu d'Art Contemporani de Barcelona in 1996 with the title "Views of the Museum".

Each artist contributed their own personal vision of the Museum. Magdalena Jeletová chose to use the building itself, designed by the American, Richard Meier, as the material for her contribution. Cutting the building up into unequal parts and dispersing it throughout the city of Barcelona means that the architecture is not seen as a monolithic monument but as an element which is questionable in its context. The building is converted into a spectacle in its own right, into an absurd part of the scenery.

Each fragment taken from the building functions as an element of shock, as a mechanism for interrupting reality. The pieces become parasites which occupy unusual sites in the city where their psychological meanings, both absurd and recognizable, can be judged and where the new sites have the capacity to restore to each fragment its own functional capacity and basic meaning. Balconies in the subway tunnels, slabs appearing like beds in the street, benches floating in the port or hydraulic brakes for trains in a station are seen as fragments which emerge with their brutal formal strength reinforced.

A line traced by laser separates the American
and Eurasian continents. The Atlantic
Ocean Range becomes visible for over
220 miles as it crosses Iceland, following,
measuring and tracing a line which divides
the island in two, running between geysers
over the abrupt terrain thrown up by the Chain.

ICELAND PROJECT

Location: Iceland.

Date: 1992.

Photograph: Werner Hannappel.

The remains of bunkers used in
World War II, abandoned, deteriorating
and attacked by the force of the waves of
the North Sea hitting the Danish coast.
A series of words projected by laser speak
to us of what has occurred there and what is
yet to happen. The beach and its memories
act as the stage for the word.

ATLANTIK-WALL

Location: Jutland, Denmark.

Date: 1994-1995.

Photograph: Werner Hannappel.

THE BATTLE AGAINST TELLURIC AND COSMIC FORCES

AN EMPTY ARK OR A LITTLE TEMPLE WARMS THE CUP

A building that is the setting for itself. Returning the value of its context to the architecture by dividing it into parts. The shell of the building is broken up into pieces and dispersed around the city. Each piece appears as an unusual parasite of the context in which it is placed. They function as elements which interrupt the established order and in this way some of their real significance as functional objects is returned to them.

DISLOCATIONS

Location: Museu d'Art Contemporani de Barcelona, Spain.

Date: 1996.

Andy Goldsworthy

Storm King Wall - Fielgate - Road Stone - Herring Island

Andy Goldsworthy has spent years working in and with nature. His work centers around a return to the free, direct experience of the environment which man has slowly relinquished in his eagerness to take tighter control of his surroundings. Yet it is precisely our awareness of this ever increasing control that allows us to truly appreciate a body of work of this kind. Andy Goldsworthy concentrates his work in the gaps between world focuses of economic activity, in barren landscapes where our mind comes into direct contact with what today are merely remnants of pre-industrial landscapes.

Goldsworthy's work deals with the experience he supposes to have existed in the days when man lived side-by-side with his environment in a kind of collaboration rather than an attempt to dominate it. Direct contact with the elements and natural phenomena, the qualities of materials, gravity, all seem to have been left on the wayside to the modern-day experience. Only artists and children are capable of recreating. It is in these pre-industrial landscapes that the personal history of the artist and his awareness of the surroundings recreate life, the need to touch things once again, but not with the hands of a child who grew up in rural England; this time he feels the resistance of the place, the elements, the materials and time, and filters them through his reflections as an adult artist.

He works directly with materials from the immediate environment, avoiding all contact with the mutations that tools represent, and using traditional building techniques. The works we present here pick up the artist's well-known childhood images, the dichotomy between our perception of nature and the use we make of it. Man constructs limits, separating the things which appear to have none. It is ownership of the land and its division that concern him: the absurdity of marking out limits in a forest, drawing out lines to separate in two, the perplexity of coming up against a wall in the middle of the woods.

Storm King Wall in New York State stands amidst a plantation of trees. It is a stone wall, like those traditionally built to mark boundaries, weaving in and out of the trees to create the plantation boundary. It expresses the irony and absurdity of man-made divisions within a forest, a limit which breaks with the rationality which is supposedly part of land ownership and everything that is planted on it. The perplexity is now two-fold, the result not just of the division, but of the boundary itself. **Fieldgate**, also in the state of New York, takes the same subject as its theme. A fragment of wall which does not actually separate anything but leaves a gap, like a gate, as if there were something different on the other side. Here, the hand of man is superposed onto nature's work. The wall is built along a fallen tree, altering its natural position on the ground. The length of the wall that does not separate anything is dictated by the length of the tree rather than any concern as to ownership of the land. In spite of the familiarity of this type of construction, the object and its location always leave people somewhat perplexed. **Road Stone** rests on existing boundary walls; here again we have a wall superposed onto something that already exists. A great rock is trapped by a wall, but not in a natural position. A little intervention, lifting the rock a hand's height above the ground, reproduces this strange perplexity. Finally, we also include an Australian project: **Herring Island**, near Melbourne. A stretch of retaining wall, apparently rendered unnecessary by the natural bank of earth, conceals a large rock in a hole, like a grotto in an Italian garden. A collection of stones are carefully piled up to form an egg-shape; a completely foreign body appears in the middle of the forest, and perplexity comes to the fore once again.

On the previous page:
The irony of an absurd division of a copse
of trees. A snaking wall separates
the last file of trees.

STORM KING WALL

Location: New York State, U.S.A.

Date: 1997.

Photograph: Andy Goldsworthy.

A huge rock trapped in the wall.
A hand's-width separates it from the ground.
Why has such effort been used to lift
the rock and leave it in exactly this spot?

ROAD STONE

Location: Kisco, New York, U.S.A.

Date: 1996.

Photograph: Andy Goldsworthy.

A boundary wall which does not enclose anything. It is just as long as a fallen tree. A gate which separates nothing in the middle of a great wood.

FIELDGATE

Location: Poundridge, New York, U.S.A.

Date: 1993.

Photograph: Andy Goldsworthy.

A rock placed inside a cave in a short stretch of retaining wall. The stones are patiently, carefully piled up, defying gravity, to create a strange stone egg in the middle of the forest.

HERRING ISLAND

Location: Melbourne, Australia.

Date: 1997.

Photograph: Andy Goldsworthy.

Enric Batlle

1956. Born in Barcelona, Spain.
Graduated in Architecture from the Barcelona School of Architecture (ETSAB). Graduate in Landscape Architecture. Lecturer in Landscape Architecture at El Vallès School of Architecture (ETSAV), Spain, and on the master's degree course in Landscape Architecture at the Universitat Politècnica de Catalunya.
He has worked with Joan Roig since 1981 in their Barcelona studio.

Eduard Bru

Born in Barcelona, Spain.
1975. Graduated in Architecture.
1987. Doctor of Architecture.
Full-time lecturer in Projects at the Barcelona School of Architecture (ETSAB).
1980-1990. Member of the editorial board of *Quaderns d'Arquitectura*, the official journal of the Catalan Architects' Association.

Burton Associates

Wm. S. Burton

1976. Graduated in Science and Ornamental Horticulture from the California Polytechnic State University, San Luis Obispo, California, USA.
1977. Master in Agricultural Sciences from the same university.
1981-1989. Worked for Roger DeWeese Inc. & Associates. As of 1985 he has held the post of vice president.
1989. Founder and president of Burton Associates. Wm S. Burton's associates are Abbie Druliner and Keith Mittemeyer.

Santiago Calatrava Valls

1951. Born in Benimanet, Valencia, Spain.
1974. Graduated in Architecture from the Valencia School of Architecture, Spain.
1979. Qualified as Civil Engineer from the Federal Swiss Institute of Technology (ETH), Zurich.
1981. Doctor of Architecture from the ETH, Zurich. Set up his studio in Zurich.
Doctor Honoris Causa from the Polytechnic University of Valencia, Spain; University of Seville, Spain; Herriot-Watt University, Edinburgh, Scotland and Salford University College, England.

Gilles Clément

Born on 6 October 1943.
1967. Engineer from the ENSH (Versailles).
1969. Landscape Architect from the DPLG (Versailles).
Lecturer at the Versailles School of Architecture.
Garden designer since 1976.

Bruno Fortier

Qualified as an architect from the DPLG.
Graduated from the Paris Urban Development Institute.

1989. Grand Prix of criticism.
He works as an architect in Paris with Jean-Thierry Bloch, an engineer qualified at the École Central de Paris.

Paul-Armand Gette

1927. Born in Lyons on 13 May.
Interested in mineralogy and petrography since the age of 7, expressed in his reading and family museum visits.
Since 1956 he has worked in very varying fields: articles, publications, exhibitions, film, etc., mainly in France and Germany.

Andy Goldsworthy

1956. Born in Cheshire, United Kingdom.
1974-1975. Studied at Bradford Art College.
1975-1978. Completed his art studies at Preston Polytechnic, Lancaster.
He has exhibited his work in countries such as the USA, Japan, Australia, Germany, France, the United Kingdom and Belgium.
He received an honorary title from the University of Bradford in 1993 for his work and was named Member of Honor of the University of Central Lancashire in 1995.

Monika Gora

1978-1983. Graduated in Landscape Architecture from the Swedish University of Agriculture, Upsala. Member of the Swedish Association of Landscape Architects (LAR) and the Swedish Artists' Association (KRO).
1981-1983. Worked in Holland as an associate architect.
1987. Studied in London.
1988. She set up her own studio, GORA art&landscape ab, and since then has carried out numerous projects and installations in Sweden and abroad.

Hargreaves Associates

George Hargreaves

1976. Completed his studies in Landscape Architecture at the University of Georgia School of Environmental Design, USA.
1979. Master of Landscape Architecture, Harvard University Graduate School of Design, Cambridge, Massachusetts, USA.
1991-1996. Lecturer in the Department of Landscape Architecture, Harvard University Graduate School of Design, Cambridge Massachusetts, USA. He has been director of this Department since 1996.
Hargreaves Associates, founded in 1983 by G. Hargreaves, has branches in San Francisco, California and Cambridge, Massachusetts devoted to the creation of landscape architecture projects.

Jordi Henrich

1957. Born in Barcelona, Spain.
1982. Graduated in Architecture from the Barcelona School of Architecture (ETSAB).
1985. Master's degree in Architecture from the University of Columbia, New York.
Architect at the Urban Project Service of Barcelona City Council.

Magdalena Jetelová

1946. Born in Semily, Czech Republic.
1965-1967. Studied at the Akademie der Bildenden Künste, Prague, Czech Republic.
1967-1968. Continued her studies at the Accademia di Brera, Milan, Italy.
1968-1971. Completed her studies at the Akademie der Bildenden Künste, Prague.
1985. Emigrated to the German Federal Republic.
Since 1990 she has been a lecturer at the Staatliche Kunstakademie, Düsseldorf.
Since 1992, she has been a Member of Honor of the Akademie der Künste, Berlin.
Her work has been exhibited in many European countries (Czech Republic, Germany, the United Kingdom, Austria, Slovenia, Ireland, Denmark, Iceland, Spain, Belgium, France, Hungary, Portugal), the USA, Canada and Australia.

Elmar Knippschild

Born in Ostwig, Germany. He studied Gardening and Landscape in Berlin, graduating in 1978.
1979-1997. Worked in collaboration with C. Müller and J. Wehberg.
In 1997 he set up as Knippschild-Simons in Berlin.

Luc Lampaert

1964. Born on 17 January.
Graduated in Landscape Architecture in 1989 from the Melle Horticulture School, Belgium.
Guest student of the Royal Academy of Fine Arts (Landscape Department).
1993. He set up his own studio.
Since 1994 he has been a member of the Belgian Association of Landscape Architects (BVTL).
1996. He has been co-editor of the journal *Groen Venster*, the bulletin of the BVTL.

Bernard Lassus

Student at the Fernand Léger Workshop and the School of Fine Arts, Paris.
1968. Started lecturing at the same school.
1976-1986. Lecturer at the National Landscape School, Versailles.
1986. Director of the post-graduate course "Gardens, Landscapes, Territories" at La Villette School of Architecture, Paris.
1996. Grand Prix National du Paysage.

Latz & Partner

1968. The firm was set up in Aachen and Saarbrücken.
1973. The Aachen branch moved to Kassel.
1988. The main office was set up in the Munich region.
In addition to Anneliese, Peter and Tilman Latz, another 15 landscape architects work at Latz & Partners at the various branches in Kranzberg, Duisberg and Potsdam.

Peter Latz

1964. Qualified as an Engineer from the Technische Universität München.
1968. Continued his studies at the Urban Development Department of the RWTH Aachen.
1968-1973. Speaker at the Amsterdam and Maastricht Architecture Academies.
Since 1983 Lecturer in Landscape Architecture at the Technische Universität München-Weihenstephan.

Anneliese Latz.

1963. Graduated as a Landscape Architect from the Technische Universität München.
Since 1968 she has worked as a landscape architect.

Tilman Latz

1993. Qualified as a Landscape Architect from the University of Kassel.
1997. Graduated in Architecture from the University of Kassel.
Has worked for the firm Latz & Partner since 1993.

Fumihiko Maki

1928. Born in Tokyo, Japan.
1952. Graduated in Architecture from the University of Tokyo.
Lecturer at the University of Washington (1956-1961), Harvard University (1962-1965) and Tokyo University (1979-1989).
He has received various international awards, including the Japan Institute of Architecture Award (1985), the Wolf Prize (1988), the Pritzker Prize (1993) and the UIA Gold Medal (1993).

José Antonio Martínez Lapeña

1941. Born in Tarragona, Spain.
1962. Graduated as a Technical Architect.
1968. Qualified as an Architect from the Barcelona School of Architecture (ETSAB).
Since 1983 he has been Lecturer in Projects at El Vallès School of Architecture (ETSAV).
Professional partnership with Elias Torres since 1968.

Desmond Muirhead

Born in England and graduate from the University of Cambridge, he is president of the planning studies firm Desmond Muirhead Inc., based in Newport Beach, Florida, and Tokyo which creates urban planning projects for important firms all over the world. One specialty for which he is recognized is golf course design, which he always develops personally with the incorporation of creative criteria. Desmond Muirhead is considered to be an atypical architect-entrepreneur because he develops projects personally without the help of assistants.

Cornelia Müller

Born in Osnabrück, Germany. Studied Gardening and Landscape in Berlin, graduating in 1977.
1979-1997. She has worked in collaboration with J. Wehberg and E. Knippschild in Berlin.
In 1997, together with J. Wehberg, she set up the studio Lützow 7 in Berlin, where they concentrate their professional praxis.

Hiroshi Nakao

Born in Kobe, Japan.
1989. Graduated in Architecture from the University of Tsukuba.
Since 1989 he has worked independently in his own professional studio.

Joan Roig

1954. Born in Barcelona, Spain.
Graduated in Architecture from the Barcelona School of Architecture (ETSAB). Lecturer in Projects at the Barcelona School of Architecture and on the master's degree course in Landscape Architecture at the Universitat Politècnica de Catalunya. Guest lecturer at Washington University, St. Louis, Missouri in 1995. He has worked with Enric Batlle since 1981 in their Barcelona studio.

Martha Schwartz

1973. Completed her studies in Fine Art at the University of Michigan, USA.
1974-1976. Master's degree in Landscape Architecture, University of Michigan, Ann Arbor, USA.
1976-1977. Landscape Architecture Program, Harvard University Graduate School of Design, Massachusetts, USA.
1990. After working with landscape architects Peter Walker, Ken Smith and David Meyer, she set up her own firm, Martha Schwartz Inc. in San Francisco, California, USA.
She has been guest lecturer at many universities in North America, Europe and Australia. She is currently assistant lecturer on the Landscape Architecture course at Harvard Graduate School of Design, Cambridge, Massachusetts, USA.

Alvaro Siza Vieira

1933. Born in Matosinhos, Portugal.
1955. Graduated in Architecture from the Architecture Faculty, Universidade de Porto, Portugal.
1955-1958. Worked in the studio of architect Fernándo Távora.
1988. Mies van der Rohe Prize, Barcelona.
1992. Pritzker Prize from the Hyatt Foundation, Chicago.
Since 1966 Lecturer in the Architecture Faculty, Universidade de Porto, Portugal.
Doctor Honoris Causa from the University of Valencia, Spain and the École Polytechnique Fédérale in Lausanne, Switzerland. Guest lecturer at many universities in Europe, the USA and South America.

Preben Skaarup

Born in 1946. Studied Architecture at the Aarhus School of Architecture, Denmark, where he has been an associate lecturer since 1975. Between 1980 and 1982 he was editor of *Landskab*, the leading landscape architecture journal in Denmark. In 1984, he set up his own studio and is currently working on architecture for gardens, cemeteries, parks and other landscape projects.

Olga Tarrasó

1956. Born in Navarrès, Valencia, Spain.
1982. Graduated in Architecture from the Barcelona School of Architecture (ETSAB).
1985. Master's degree in Architecture from the University of Columbia, New York.
Architect at the Urban Project Service of Barcelona City Council.

Elias Torres Tur

1944. Born in Ibiza, Spain.
1968. Graduated in Architecture from the Barcelona School of Architecture (ETSAB)
1993. Doctor of Architecture from the ETSAB.
Since 1979 he has been a lecturer in Landscape Architecture at the ETSAB.
Since 1996, he has been a full-time lecturer in Projects at the ETSAB.
Since 1968 he has worked in professional partnership with José Antonio Martínez Lapeña.

Jan Wehberg

Born in Osnabrück, Germany. Studied Gardening and Landscape in Berlin, graduating in 1978.
1979-1997. Worked in collaboration with C. Müller and E. Knippschild in Berlin.
In 1997, together with C. Müller, he set up the Lützow 7 studio in Berlin where they concentrate their professional praxis.

West 8

Group of landscape architects set up in 1987 in Rotterdam.
They develop projects for a variety of fields: landscape architecture, urban design, public space and industrial design.